The Ginger Tree

THE GINGER TREE
Christopher Hampton

Adapted from
the novel by Oswald Wynd

faber and faber
LONDON · BOSTON

First published in 1989
by Faber and Faber Limited
3 Queen Square London WC1N 3AU

Photoset by Wilmaset Birkenhead Wirral
Printed in Great Britain by
Richard Clay Ltd Bungay Suffolk

A CIP record of this book is available from the British Library

ISBN 0-571-14181-1

For Alice and Mary

CONTENTS

INTRODUCTION
The Ginger Tree – a Japanese Diary

I began work on The Ginger Tree *in 1985 and travelled out to Tokyo in May to join Alan Shallcross, Executive Producer for the BBC, for a series of meetings at NHK (the Japanese state broadcasting company) and to spend a few days on my own researches. What follows is the journal I kept on that visit, interrupted by whatever explanatory amplifications have been made necessary by the many vicissitudes of a four-year international co-production.*

18 MAY The plane was full and I was in the centre block between two Japanese, both of whom engaged me briefly in conversation. On my right said he was in security: evidently good at this, since he gave no further details whatsoever. On my left didn't speak until the film (a preposterous farrago starring Michael Caine, Laurence Olivier and my old friend Charles Gray as a bald homosexual traitor), when he asked me the meaning of 'jigsaw'. I explained as best I could. In that case, what was a 'jigsaw man'? Further explanation. This seemed to do the trick, for by the end of the credit titles he was, enviably, fast asleep. Man on my right was an astonishing drinker: champagne, red wine, brandy, beer and, above all, scotch was put back uninterruptedly from London to Tokyo, without visible effect.

We put down at Anchorage, a bizarre stopover amidst some serious-looking mountains. A stuffed polar bear dominated the duty-free area. On the second leg of the flight I dozed off for an hour or so and was woken by a dawn chorus of angry crickets: this turned out to be dozens of Japanese shaving with squash-ball-sized miniature battery razors.

I was met at Narita by Mr Naonori Kawamura of NHK and driven to Tokyo, a journey of almost two hours. First the motorway cuts through pleasant countryside, past groups of conifers huddled close together, as if aware that space is very limited. Then, glimpses of sea and mudflats. Slow two-lane traffic crawls across the river and into the city; weird effect of expressways being a storey or two above ground or else plunging into tunnels, so that one didn't see a single pedestrian for over an hour.

Then, as we descended to the street where the Hotel Tobu stands, the pavements are suddenly packed with people.

Mr K takes me out for a tempura dinner: delicious. He explains what a strain Western eating is for him: in Japan, he says, the custom is to eat in silence and he finds the necessity to make conversation unsettling. This ties in with a warning given to me by Tim Rice, who complained of long Japanese meals in painful silence. We discuss, in so far as Mr K's English permits, cultural differences.

Back at the hotel I call home and turn on the TV. The first image is Johnny Cash, dressed as a priest, delivering a sermon in Japanese: on another channel, Peter Sellers does his Japanese Clouseau. I muse on how they manage the French accent in the dubbing. The room is very small, the bed is on the diagonal; but it's comfortable enough. Free day tomorrow.

At 8.30 this evening there were vast crowds on the street. Everybody looked amazingly young. I commented on this and Mr K explained that this was because they were young. The street we're in, Koendori in Shibuya, is the favoured beat of 'young man and young lady', according to Mr K, the most fashionable shopping street in Japan.

19 MAY Woke at 3.30 and could only doze fitfully thereafter. Breakfasted at 9.00 and then set off for what turned out to be a five-hour walk. First I went down the hill to Shibuya station, intending to travel to the north-east of Tokyo to Asakusa, where there is meant to be a festival on this date at the Asakusa Kannon Temple. The Ginza line was what I needed. However, after wandering about for some time in the enormous station precincts, passing chanting schoolchildren and many other large and purposeful groups, I retired baffled and walked back up past the hotel to go instead to the Meiji Shrine (two stars in Baedeker) in the Yoyoga Park. After only one wrong turning I found it, and visited first the Imperial Garden (the irises in the famous line of beds are unfortunately not out for a couple of weeks), then the shrine itself and finally (a long walk and a melancholy little museum) the Treasury.

Episodes 2 and 3 of the series are set during the Meiji era, during which the Emperor Meiji (who died in 1912) opened the country up to Western trade and influence, making enterprises like Mary Mackenzie's possible for the first time.

At the shrine I stood among crowds who applaud loudly before praying and throw small change into huge coffers, and watched a mass baptism ceremony. This began with a deafening blow to a huge drum, which miraculously failed to make any of the infants (all in elaborate white lace) cry. The senior priest prayed, a junior priest waved a kind of white stick with paper streamers, a woman in an exquisite kimono shook a cluster of bells (my camera jammed at this point) and the junior priest distributed to each father a spray of leaves (which looked suspiciously shiny, perhaps more plastic than plastic itself). These were left behind and collected up afterwards. The priests wear ferocious-looking shiny black clogs, which I calculated might be even more lethal than my new espadrilles. After the ceremony a wedding procession crossed the shrine, the bride in fantastically elaborate costume and make-up and the groom in black, attended by two or three dozen men in black suits, making it seem as if the bride in her reds and yellows and big white hat with flowers hadn't been told the sad news. Elsewhere two girl children in kimonos and full make-up were being professionally photographed.

The long detour to the Treasury museum (simply some photographs of the Emperor Meiji and his wife and a few of their effects in glass cases) had tired me and I was thinking longingly of a beer and some sushi, when I became aware that the road, where earlier I had taken a wrong turning, was now jam-packed with pedestrians and giving off a sound like the history of the discothèque. It's the street where Japanese teenagers come, every Sunday, to jive, jitterbug, breakdance and generally cavort. At one end, under the pedestrian bridge, a mime artist plied his trade (changing, every so often, under a blanket), but after him came the groups of dancers, chronologically organized. It started with the fifties, youths with fantastic greased quiffs and girls in taffeta dresses and bobby-sox; then, as I progressed down the street, there was reggae (here I was impressed by two boys in traditional Japanese costume, heavily made up and immaculately rehearsed); breakdancing (they spun on their heads on strips of cardboard, but tended to fall over afterwards); and eventually spectacular roller disco with acrobatic stunts performed either without mechanical aids or else behind some contraption like an automatic unicycle or land jet-ski. The crowds were amiable, with the exception of a group of rockers, who threw Coke cans at two Americans, who were causing annoyance by bumping into the dancers as they filmed. What with one thing and another, it was almost 4.00 by the time I arrived back at the Tobu.

I turned on the TV in time to catch the Emperor's arrival at the Sumo championships, which are happening this week in Tokyo. There was a surrealistic image of this frail old boy, looking pretty much like E. M. Forster, blowing and sucking his way determinedly through the foyer, shot from behind a row of immensely fat, almost naked men, bowing deeply. Later he perches on a giant chair, the back of which rears up far above his head, watching intently as these massive parties square up, grunting powerfully, delicately adjusting the row of spikes at either hip as they squat, and eventually charging each other like maddened elephants. Lulled by this, I fell asleep, to be woken at 6.00 by a Mr Takeshi Nakazato calling from reception, inviting me to a cup of tea while we waited for the imminent arrival of Marilyn Hall from Los Angeles.

Marilyn Hall was the Canadian producer (based in Los Angeles) who, with her partner Juliet Gitterman in New York, had originally bought the rights to Oswald Wynd's novel. Finally, no doubt battered by years of delay and disappointment, she was to withdraw from the project.

Mr N dealt a blow to my sushi plan by explaining that sushi on a Sunday (the only day the fish market at Tsukiji doesn't function) was not a good idea. He diagnosed my failure at Shibuya station by pointing out that the Ginza line departs from the third floor: this hadn't occurred to me. However, I didn't regret the way the day had turned out. Time passed and an announcement arrived: Marilyn's plane was going to be three hours late. As we waited, my stomach miraculously not rumbling, Mr N outlined next week's schedule. There's to be a three-day script conference in Hakone (this sounds ominous) and trips are to be arranged to Kyoto, Nara, Osaka, Nikko and Karuizawa. But his most pressing concern was to find out what I wished to do tomorrow. I couldn't think of anything and, it seemed, neither could he. Being left alone was tentatively suggested but decisively rejected. In the end, inspiration failing, we agreed to discuss it in the morning. Marilyn arrived, we went to the tempura bar in the basement and I had precisely the same (delicious) meal as last night.

20 MAY Mr N phones around 10.00 and briskly offers three alternatives for the day: (1) I should go and see a Hong Kong Chinese film, a historical extravaganza shot in Peking on the very locations we might hope to use in the first episode; (2) I should report to NHK for a tour of the studios; (3) I should return to the station and take my subway from the third floor. I choose (1). Mr N seems a little winded by this.

It's been raining most of the night and continues to spit as I make my way to the Palace Cinema. The film is in Chinese with Japanese subtitles and deals, as far as I can make out, with the youth of the Dowager Empress in the 19th century. A mere concubine, she catches the Emperor's attention with the well-known handkerchief-into-mouse trick, but to her mortification he chooses another (his wife appears to be chosen by lot, but I may have misunderstood this). The Emperor is at war with Britain (represented by a number of Chinese extras with yellow beards) and in subsequent negotiations, comic relief is provided when the British envoy, vainly sticking to the Queensberry rules, is trounced by a younger man and thrown into a pond. This results in the sack of Peking, with the British in the role of the villainous barbarians, raping, looting etc. The Emperor retires with his court to a summer palace, where the Dowager Empress-to-be lurks about inconspicuously in a hat the size of an accordion, until she succeeds in arousing the Emperor's interest by singing the first line of a song and then running to a distant pavilion before completing it. It's the senior wife, however, who has the baby. The rest of the film concerns itself with court intrigue. Three moustachioed counsellors, indistinguishable in fringed topees like lampshades, and a junior concubine plot against the Dowager Empress. The Emperor is in poor health and has a tendency to pass out in theatres. Eventually he dies, appointing his two wives as joint regents (the Dowager Empress has the edge here, because she can read). There's a confrontational meeting (at which the moustaches come on so strong the Crown Prince, who's about eight, pisses himself) and the Dowager Empress decides to show her hand (by now her nails are about a foot long and her hat has more beads hanging off it than the entrance to a Turkish coffee-shop). She has her enemies arrested. Moustache 1, prevented from speaking at last by a dinky device popped into his mouth, is pelted with a good deal of fruit and veg. and beheaded; Moustache 2, invited to hang himself, reluctantly complies; and Moustache 3 is smothered with surprising speed by a number of wet handkerchiefs. In a climactic final scene, the Dowager Empress has a conversation with the remains of her rival, now contained in a jar of modest proportions. It's a conversation which appears to displease her.

The locations are spectacular; let's hope NHK's negotiations with Chinese TV, presently taking place, are successful.

They were not. I wrote the first episode, setting it in Peking as agreed, but a year later Naonori Kawamura explained to me at a meeting at the BBC that the location would have to be changed to avoid affronting Chinese sensibilities. The Chinese, it appeared, had a blanket objection to any treatment of this late Imperial period – an objection they managed to overcome in the case of Bertolucci, but let that pass – and the Japanese were not disposed to offend them. They suggested I relocate the episode in Hong Kong. This seemed not to be a good idea, since the Hong Kong of the period was a comfortable colonial outpost, lacking the remoteness and isolation I required. We haggled. Wei-haiwei (a port on mainland China administered at this period by the British) and Formosa were no more acceptable to the Chinese than Peking; while Korea, on the other hand, was too sore a point to the Japanese. Finally we compromised, as I'd hoped we might, on Manchuria. This was the battle-ground of the Russian–Japanese war, a far more appropriate curtain-raiser than the Boxer Rising in Peking to the era which culminated in Pearl Harbor, in the sense that the Japanese victory over their corrupt and arrogant European antagonist profoundly redefined the Japanese self-image.

The American contribution to these 1986 discussions was to ask me to expand the script, for reasons connected with scheduling and advertising slots, from 240 to 260 minutes: this gave me the opportunity to deal with the Russian–Japanese war in some detail. Later, back at 240 minutes, this material was to disappear again, for financial as well as timing reasons. I began to understand why the word 'co-production' strikes such dread into the hearts of my more experienced colleagues.

The vending machine outside my room dispenses an excellent drink, unappealingly called SWEAT, a kind of lemon squash made with ionized water: I spend all my spare change on this.

I took a walk round the area in the warm evening rain. The immense press of people in the streets fosters a curious illusion: that if one were to stop to look in a shop window, the whole of central Tokyo might grind to a halt. The thought kept me moving.

Alan Shallcross arrived at about 8.30 and we ate in the hotel coffee shop, which provides a kind of BBC or school food. I had a minute steak, in both senses of the term, making it three meals today in the lobby. Sushi seems easier to come by in London. Another stroll in the rain with Alan and a fearsomely expensive nightcap in the bar. A last glass of SWEAT and so to bed.

21 MAY Long, gruelling and rainy day. Reported to NHK at 10.00 and first met, in a spectacular twentieth-floor office overlooking the Yoyogi Park and downtown Tokyo, Mr Mikio Kawaguchi, one of the managing directors. He was impressively late; then we sat at a round table for tea, Messrs K and N hovering in the background, and our birdlike interpreter, whose rather beautiful name she told us to abbreviate to Sam, doing the honours. Alan was extremely diplomatic. Mr Kawaguchi asked me how long I had been a professional writer: the reply enabled him to opine unflatteringly that I must only be in my forties.

I was in my thirties.

A few floors down, in Mr K's section of the open-plan office, we were joined by our researcher, Shunsuke Katori, a fresh-faced youth whose rare contributions to our discussions never rose above a bashful murmur and who subsequently turned out to be in his forties. Finally, we descended to the studios in the basement to watch rehearsals for one of the daily soaps.

After a delicious lunch which we ate sitting cross-legged on the floor, our party (five Anglos and six Japanese) climbed into a coach and set off to Kamakura, a wealthy suburb of Tokyo close to the beach, and apparently the only feasible location in the Tokyo area. We were taken to the Shinto shrine and admired a giant statue of Buddha. Later we wandered down side roads, looking at potential houses. We found one, unoccupied, which I imagine might do very well for Mary's first house at Tsukiji. Our hosts seemed politely sceptical. We moved on to the Bluff at Yokohama, where there are still one or two period houses, which however look down across a vast and noisy shipyard. Nothing really usable.

In fact, we shot in neither of these locations.

Finally, an excellent Chinese meal in Yokohama. I drank beer and warm Chinese sake (which is brownish, taken with sugar and tastes not unlike Bovril). Even at the time this seemed an unwise combination. The food ranged from delicious (shark's fin soup) through mysterious (a gelatinous mass not even the Japanese could identify, served with a quail's egg) to alarming (jellyfish, sea slug). Then the long drive back.

22 MAY Most exhausting day so far. The meeting at NHK lasted from 10.00 to 5.30 (with a lunch break) and consisted of my putting the case for my version of the plot. If they agreed, they said so; if not, a ghastly silence would fall and no question from us, however direct, would be answered. By the end of the day we had more or less worked through all four episodes and I felt I'd been through a wringer.

Dinner at a French restaurant (three stars in the Japanese Michelin) and we stumbled home.

Present today for the first time was Ken Miyamoto, the Japanese playwright, friend and translator of Arnold Wesker, who is to be my adviser and will translate the large amount of Japanese dialogue I envisage. His face is scored with experience, he looks physically frail but mentally tough and his sense of humour is in full working order.

Ken Miyamoto died before the project finally got under way; I benefited greatly from his advice and experience.

23 MAY 2.30 a.m.: Too tired and drunk to do this.

24 MAY What happened last night was that we took them out: to an Italian restaurant in Roppongi, where, after another long day in the smoke-filled room, in which as in some nightmare everyone began to reiterate all the things they'd said on Wednesday morning

(the 22nd), I hit the Chianti fairly enthusiastically. At a certain point Ken asked if I would accompany him to a bar after dinner and I said it sounded good to me. We set off on foot, accompanied by Mr K. The bar proved to be a kind of gentleman's club, front room with a bar and tables and back room with sofas and all the regulars' bottles of whisky, each in its separate compartment. The two available drinks seemed to be Japanese scotch and a poison-ous-looking colourless local brew drunk with hot water. We took a table on which stood a bottle of scotch, two bottles of soda, a full ice-bucket, a thermos for the hot water, and two carafes of the colourless liquid. I felt it safer to plump for scotch. However, the method is that no sooner do you take a sip than the glass is instantly refilled. This makes it extremely difficult to nurse a drink. I was startled by the fact that one of the first things to catch my eye was a photograph of my late friend, the actor Victor Henry: the bar was full of English and American theatre posters, one of which was Arnold Wesker's *The Friends*, with photos of all the cast.

In due course, the owner of the bar appeared, a distinguée lady of a certain age and in no time we were gossiping about her friends in the English theatre, Arnold and Dusty, Michael Bogdanov, Howard Davies. We drank and talked and drank and drank. Eventually Miyamoto-san, who had been taking alternate slugs of both available beverages, left the room for some time. On his return, he fell over. Shortly thereafter he stumbled off home, and Mr K who had been sipping a discreet soda-water throughout, took me home, where I enjoyed, I must say, by far the best night's sleep I'd had since I arrived.

The hangover, though severe, was not as brutal or incapacitat-ing as I had feared (since I hadn't drunk scotch for five years or more) and by the first meeting at 11 o'clock (to discuss next week's schedule with Mr N), I was feeling perfectly all right, indeed rather chipper. The discussion followed a now-familiar pattern: my proposals immediately dismissed as quite impractical, followed by long and patient negotiations leading to a compromise slightly favouring my position. Thus, I say I would like to stay one more week in order to visit Nikko and Karuizawa (locations in the novel): he responds that I cannot of course hope to achieve this in a week when they had counted on having me for at least two, and adds that since the scenes in Nikko in the novel are very bad and it is impossible to film in Karuizawa, I must put these places out of my mind and instead go to Nara, Nagoya, Osaka, Kyoto and Hakone, spending several days at each. Prolonged haggling. Finally, we agree that I shall stay on nine days and visit Nikko, Nara, Kyoto and Hakone. Karuizawa remains a sore point, although I tell him I'm perfectly prepared to go on my own.

Around 12.30 we arrived at the Kabuki Theatre. When we went in, it had already been going for ninety minutes and was due to continue until 4.00 p.m. It turned out to be wonderful. The actors, all male, have been passing their roles on from generation to generation since the sixteenth century, drawing from a repertoire of about 2,000 plays. The star of this show is Danjuro XII. There were earphones with simultaneous translation, but I preferred simply to watch. It was entirely comprehensible. The first piece was almost all sung by the four singers accompanied by three samisen players and was a three-handed journey piece about a young man and his bride-to-be fleeing to her parents. He's exceedingly depressed, but she persuades him not to kill himself; later he rouses himself sufficiently to defend her against a buffoonish bandit, whose ten soldiers he defeats in stylized battle. The sounds made by both singers and actors are quite unearthly. The visual effects (on a wide Cinemascope stage) are breathtaking. In the next play, Danjuro (in a vast costume with stilts, trailing trouser-legs and sleeves like hang-gliders, which have to be arranged in the middle of the play by four stage-hands before he can go into battle) plays a passing knight who saves a young couple from execution (the actor playing the wicked governor has been declared a Living National Treasure by Act of Parliament) and in the most spectacular effect cuts the heads off ten of his opponents with one stroke of his mighty sword. I was most reluctant to leave, just after the beginning of the final play, which opened in much the same way as its predecessor – curtain drawn back by hand, brief forestage business with extras, then, in a ravishing effect, a second, plain curtain pulled away downwards to reveal the entire company in spectacular costumes in front of highly coloured, framed, painted sets, and finally the entrance of the leading actor down a catwalk built through the stalls. The audience, apparently extremely knowledgeable, comes and goes, chats animatedly, eats lunch, drinks, laughs and applauds favourite moments. Many of the women, especially the older ones, wear kimonos, the first time I've seen this in a public place.

A period of some chaos ensued. It was now pouring with rain and Mr N didn't appear until the moment the theatre emptied. Tago-san, his very efficient, long-haired young assistant, was dispatched to buy us umbrellas and we climbed into three taxis to go to Tsukiji, where we were to look at the fish market and the few remaining streets of old buildings left in the city. The fish market was closed. Then some failure of coordination left Alan and me standing on a street corner under our new umbrellas in the pouring rain for half-an-hour while Mr N frantically combed the area trying to find the rest of the party. As time passed, Alan and I became hysterical with laughter. Eventually Tago appeared. Within one minute's walk of where we were standing, he led us to ideal locations: small back streets, low wooden houses, everything perfect, bar the TV aerials, the drainpipes and the occasional street light. Mr N joined us and immediately became upset, claiming people would never agree to allow their aerials to be taken down, even for ready money. There seems to be some schizophrenia at the root of this: on the one hand, the Japanese are resolutely opposed to using film, while on the other, they keep leading us to eminently suitable locations. The crunch will no doubt come tomorrow at the co-production meeting, from which I am delighted to be excluded. Alan intends to propose that the entire series be shot in Japan, and to make clear his feeling that if we cannot shoot on film (as opposed to videotape), the whole deal if off. Mr K tells me he anticipates 'big problem'.

However, after this slight contretemps, we were whisked off to a restaurant called Happo-En – an old mansion in the middle of a large and exquisite Japanese garden – for a farewell dinner (since the production team are leaving after tomorrow's meeting). Tea was served in a summerhouse and then we were taken to a private room, where we sat on the floor and ate a wonderful meal served by ladies in kimonos, while a dancer performed, accompanied by an old lady who sang and played the samisen. After this, we distributed our presents (supplied to us by the BBC). Mine to Miyamoto-san, almost as big a surprise to me as it was to him, was a heart-shaped black Wedgwood receptacle from Harrods: later, I spotted him surreptitiously removing the lid and sniffing, which left him none the wiser.

25 MAY Day off today, which I used to explore the city, departing from the subway on the third floor. Meanwhile, the negotiations were apparently extremely gruelling, revealing, among other things, that NHK have not used film for ten years. However, as I understand it, they're prepared to accommodate us on this.

I understood wrong. The series was eventually shot on (Japanese) high-definition videotape, the first series to use this method to be shown on British television. There was no location shooting in Tokyo itself.

Naonori (Mr K) came to collect me at 6.00 to take me to the première of *Kean*, a one-man show in a theatre at the top of a nearby department store, starring Emori-san, an actor recommended as a possible Kentaro Kurihama. The play was more or less impenetrable, but Emori-san was evidently a strong and witty actor.

The part of Kurihama was in fact played by the excellent Daisuke Ryu.

I was startled during the interval to discover that a gentleman sitting in front of me was the translator of one of my plays, *Total Eclipse*, the first to be performed and published in Japan. I hoped to talk to him at the party afterwards, but he wasn't there. The party itself was interesting: so many vast baskets of flowers had arrived for Emori-san the room looked like a Chicago funeral parlour. The proceedings began with speeches: from the manager of the theatre, from Emori-san (who had already made a curtain speech), from John David, the director, from his wife, Rosalind (this obviously caught her on the hop, but she coped admirably) and finally from a distinguished elderly actress. At the end of the evening, just as I was preparing to leave, everyone formed a circle and clapped their hands in rhythmic fashion: this is apparently the Japanese way of saying the party's over – on reflection it seems to me an eminently sensible arrangement.

26 MAY My first day alone here (i.e. now the producers have left) – and very interesting it was. The guide books say it's rare to be invited to a Japanese home, but Kichiro Tago arrived for me at 2.00 and took me by train to his parents' house. His father is an architect and his mother an instructress of the tea ceremony,

which she was demonstrating this afternoon. There were eight of us: Kichiro's mother, two young women (unmarried, one, with glasses), an older married woman, a seventy-five-year-old lady (the official chief guest, wearing a kimono like the other women), a young architect in a blue suit, Kichiro and I. First task is to step into the garden (in the communal garden shoes) one at a time, kneel at the well and wash the hands and mouth (thereby cleansing the heart). The ceremony itself took place in a bare room with tatami mats and paper walls, which can be closed off into a self-contained square. Against one wall there were five items: a fan, open on a stand, displaying instructions for the ceremony; a slightly dispiriting Western-style circular electric clock; an arrangement of napkins in spring colours with a lacquer box on top; an exquisite arrangement (*ikebana*) of two mauve flowers and some ferns in a slim vase; and, on the wall itself, a long thin scroll with a vertical painted line of ideograms, later identified as a poem along the lines of:

> The clouds may flow constantly past
> But the mountain remains for ever.

We arranged ourselves in an excruciating kneeling pose along two walls of the room. In the opposite corner was the apparatus for the ceremony: a circular stove on which water was already bubbling, and an arrangement of shelves housing a square pottery jug (with cold water), a wooden scoop, a lacquered tea caddy, etc. The rest of the equipment was brought in in stages by the hostess. First were squares of gelatinous pink candy in a pyramid of boxes, which was passed around and gradually deconstructed in ritual fashion, so that each person received one square, placed it on a pile of napkins and then attacked it with a pointed piece of wood, breaking it up, spearing the pieces and eating them. Then came the tea itself, in two stages I was alarmed to discover (since my thighs were already twitching and my calves were numb): strong and weak. While the rest of us wrapped up our pieces of wood in the outer napkin, the hostess prepared the strong tea in an earthenware bowl, conveying tea from the first of two caddies by means of a delicate bamboo spoon shaped like a scalpel. She then whisked the tea with an item which looks exactly like a shaving brush and passed it to the chief guest, who put it down in a designated place, looked at it, picked it up, held it in the right hand, rotated it three times with the left hand, took three slurps (noisy, but removing a minimum of liquid), turned it again and passed it on. So it went, accompanied with terrific bowing, like a loving cup or a pipe of peace. The tea itself was the consistency of mint sauce, or even tomato ketchup. As it circulated, the hostess and chief guest maintained a conversation, in which the chief guest admired, one by one, each of the decorations in the room, the bowl, the quality of the tea, while the hostess apologized profusely for the poverty of her imagination, her limited skills and the general second-rateness of the entire occasion. Around this point, I fell off my calves and resumed the agony of the kneeling position only when it was my turn to perform in the ritual. After drinking the tea, one was required to clean the rim of the bowl with another of one's napkins, before passing the bowl on. Next came more candies, followed by the weak tea, a slightly more relaxed but on the other hand more demanding stage which calls for two bowls to be in use, and the downing of the entire contents of one's bowl. Finally, the four principal items of use were circulated: the two caddies – one (for the weak tea) lacquered and decorated with children's toys, top, hobby-horse, kite; the other (for the strong tea) stone, with a round lid – the bamboo spoon; and a fabric purse in which strong tea is stored. No doubt I committed many solecisms, but the one which caused most alarm seemed to be when I touched a knob on the top of the second caddy, rather than lifting the lid off by the rim. The ceremony ended with a pleasing homage to art, as we prostrated ourselves, one by one, in front of the poem.

Supper was then served in the next room and Kichiro's father arrived from his study at the back of the house. He began by saying he knew little of the tea ceremony, but was an expert at the alcohol ceremony and went on to serve me, in what I now recognize as a Japanese custom, large quantities simultaneously of beer, vin rosé and sake. The meal was delicious, served in individual boxes, each with three shelves, each shelf containing a dish accessible when a wooden bar was removed. Thereafter (possibly for my benefit) a dish of ham and sausage and finally a bowl of soup and a bowl of rice. The beer came in large cans decorated with blue penguins, of a piece with the jolly creatures I found later, printed on the pink slippers for communal use, marked (in English) 'Toilet'.

After supper, tea was served, and rather unexpectedly as in some Victorian household, Kichiro went to the piano and a sing-song ensued. Proceedings opened with Paul McCartney's 'Yesterday' and I was later obliged to give renditions, as best I could, of 'Danny Boy', 'Auld Lang Syne', 'Land of Hope and Glory' and the national anthem, to which they responded with a number of folk songs and the Japanese anthem, for which Kichiro's father stood up. Finally, some Schubert and Beethoven before the concluding number, 'Let it Be'. After this, everyone left, including the girl with glasses (who had charmingly inquired at dinner if I was married and declared herself becomingly disappointed to hear that I was). Then Kichiro's younger sister appeared with a basket of strawberries and a pile of film programmes to show me (her room is a shrine to Alain Delon). Kichiro's father was extremely grieved to learn of the death of Vivien Leigh.

As I was leaving, they gave me two beautifully wrapped (and beautiful) presents. Thank God, I was able to produce my gift-wrapped piece of Harrod's Wedgwood in return. Messages were exchanged on thick pieces of handsome paper and Kichiro walked me to the station.

I was back at the hotel by 9.30. A genuinely fascinating day.

27 MAY Kichiro came to collect me at 8.00 and the day began with my first experience of the Tokyo subway at rush hour – not, as it turned out, as fearsome as I'd anticipated, but then it was not a heaving-in-with-the-paddles-before-the-doors-could-close kind of crowdedness. Once we got on to the train the trip to Nikko was extremely comfortable and one could feel one's spirits rise as we pulled out of the city and began to pass through rice fields (economically taking advantage of every flat surface) on the way to the mountains.

Once in Nikko we went straight for lunch (the Japanese never neglect the inner man) at a tiny restaurant split into two sections – a higher section (more popular) where the customers knelt on the tatami, and a stone-floor section with tables (where we sat). Kichiro ordered Rama-en (a kind of soup with noodles, vegetables and pieces of meat in it), preceded by dumplings containing Chinese chives. This was incredibly cheap and quite delicious. Then we visited the Toshogu shrine, which was astonishing without being particularly sympathetic. The Yomei-mon Gate, caked in gold leaf and elaborate beyond the dreams of the baroque, is no doubt very fine, but I much preferred the simplicity (once we'd clambered all the way up there) of the shrine in front of Ieyasu's tomb. Later we took a cab to the Kagon Falls, pausing to ascend by cable car to a beautiful observation point. This was virtually the only moment of the day when we were not surrounded by hordes of schoolchildren – the lift to the foot of the falls, for example, was far more brutally crammed than the subway train – and the falls were scarcely visible through the milling school parties, who seemed to be there not to look at the falls but to stand with their backs to them being photographed.

Finally we took the taxi on to Lake Chuzenji at the foot of Mt Nantai (or Mr Nantai – Nantai-san – as the Japanese whimsically prefer) where we took iced coffee in a café of unexampled hideousness. In an excellent position overlooking the lake, it had chosen to decorate itself (behind mercifully smoked glass windows) with a cherry-red and sunflower-yellow patterned carpet, heavy wooden table with elaborate bamboo chairs, hideous light fittings and, lowering over all, a ceiling lined with dark-brown crushed velvet. I fell to thinking about the extreme dichotomy in Japan between elegance – tea-ceremony, *ikebana* (the art of flower-arrangement), etc – and grotesque inelegance (pleasure-boats in the shape of ducks, illuminated clocks with cartoon characters, pink, green, or mauve beer and so on).

Kichiro's NHK money seemed to have run out, so we took a bus back to Nikko station. The road to Chuzenji is known as 'the alphabet' because of its forty-eight hairpin beds (the Japanese alphabet has forty-eight letters: this is not the half of it but that way madness lies) and what had been comfortable in a taxi was less so in a bus constructed for Japanese thighs.

On the way back to Tokyo, I continued to brood on these contrasts: elegance/inelegance; brutality/sentimentality; tranquillity/bustle. And riding through the streets (I'd splashed out on a taxi rather than going back on the subway) another contrast suggested itself. We passed through the Yoshiwara and turned into the long street of brothels, where the white neon façades light up the dozens of pairs of shoes left outside by the customers. Men in dinner-jackets and white gloves surged towards the taxi and Kichiro asked me if I would like to visit: 'Most people from London come here,' he explained. 'What about you?' I asked him, 'do you ever visit?' He looked appalled. 'Of course not,' he said. I asked him why. 'Because it costs 25,000 yen and you might get a disease.' 'Drive on,' I said; adding to my list of contrasts modesty and immodesty. And returning to the hotel through rampant neon chaos and scenes of total architectural abandon, I thought some more about the opposition between an intense instinct for disciplined taste and the complete anarchic riot of Japanese city life.

28 MAY This is more like it: the Tamahan in Kyoto – a Japanese wood, paper and tatami hotel of exceptional tranquillity and elegance, with eleven rooms arranged around a Japanese garden, away from the centre in the north of the city, below a range of wooded hills. I have one of the three upstairs rooms: a cunning piece of work, combining a traditional tatami room, where you eat and sleep, with a balcony which has chairs, a table, a fridge and a television. There's also a wonderful bathroom, of which more later; and perfect silence, except for the occasional muttering and grumbling of the fridge, from which I have just taken a bottle of something called Kbysi, with a picture of a bee on the label. It turns out to be perfectly colourless and has a strange medicinal flavour: perhaps it is actually insect repellent.

Takeshi (Mr N) and I left Tokyo this morning, again at rush hour, by the famous bullet train, boarding which involves standing in precisely the right spot on the platform, as if for some military manoeuvre. I was in slightly mutinous mood, feeling more like a location manager than a researching writer, not improved by my unwise choice from the drinks trolley of a disgusting pink concoction, served with a cocktail cherry. Takeshi chain-smoked. We got off at Nagoya, which looked deathly (apparently there are streets which could pass for turn-of-the-century Tokyo) and took a cab through the rain to Meiji-Mura, a curious and estimable project to preserve characteristic Meiji-era buildings in the form of exact reproductions beside a lake. I thought one of the houses would serve very well for Mary Mackenzie's final house on the Yokohama bluffs, but for some reason Takeshi pooh-poohed this suggestion. The site was pullulating with school parties, constantly greeting me ('haro') or taking leave of me ('bai-bai') and as it started to rain, I cut short the visit, forgetting to see Lafcadio Hearn's summerhouse or Frank Lloyd Wright's Imperial Hotel.

Mary's house in Yokohama (and half-a-dozen of the other houses) were eventually located in a place called Kurashiki, further west than I ever penetrated. Frank Lloyd Wright's hotel and the Kabuki Theatre were the locations used from the Meiji-Mura, where the production team was much troubled by school parties during filming.

Back on the train, it struck me that I genuinely had caused great interest at the site, from the taxi-driver who took us, who said foreigners hardly ever went out there, to the innumerable school-children. How much more interest must have been raised by foreigners eighty-odd years ago. All afternoon I kept hearing the word 'gaijin' (foreigner) and, given the Japanese bewilderment about what may or may not be a ginger tree, I thought this might make a more appropriate title for the series. I envisaged a scene where Mary hears the word so often, she believes it to be the Japanese for 'good morning'.

As sensitive to charges of xenophobia as the next man, the Japanese didn't care for this idea. Aside from anything else, they assured me that the correct word for the period would be 'ijin'. This didn't entirely agree with the contemporary observations of Lafcadio Hearn, but I let it pass; and eventually devised a way to get round the controversy aroused by the eponymous plant.

Kyoto, when we arrived, was bathed in brilliant sunshine, which contradicted the weather forecast, thus putting Takeshi out. I immediately felt, for the first time, the sense of a genuinely Oriental city; an impression reinforced by our arrival at the Tamahan. I was shown to my room by the maid, Kyoko, a dignified elderly woman in a kimono, whose first task was to fill the cedar-wood bath with almost boiling water and cover it with a lid. The procedure is as follows: you soap yourself, sit on a little stool, rinse yourself with basketfuls of water and only then, when you're quite clean, lower yourself into this deep, square, sweet-smelling wooden tub. The water is scalding. You sit in it (up to your neck) as long as you like or can bear and then emerge: in my case, boiled red.

We had supper in Takeshi's room – *sukiyaki*. As ever I was thrown by the absence of napkins: the chin tends to acquire a glistening crust. We sat on the floor, helped ourselves to meat and vegetables direct from the frying-pan, which are then dipped in raw egg. Meanwhile, Takeshi made a number of phone calls, as he has now kindly become preoccupied with getting me in to see *Ran*, Kurosawa's film, which is premièring at the Tokyo Film Festival.

Kyoko has now laid out my futon on the floor: to my relief, they cheat here and let you have a narrow mattress as well.

29 MAY Japanese breakfast consists of eight dishes – rice, pickles, bean curd in soy sauce, aubergine, smoked fish, omelette, deep brown soup of indeterminate variety and grapefruit. There's also a tiny pickled plum which is supposed to make the tea taste better.

A gruelling day's sightseeing (formidably organized by a garrulous elderly lady taxi-driver) began at the Sanjusangendo, the Hall of the Thirty-three Bays, which contains 1,000 not quite identical statues of the 1,000 armed Kannon (the Buddhist personification of mercy). This, while undeniably impressive, is somewhat lowering, although the long house in which it's contained is rather beautiful. Thence we sped, the rain letting up, to Nijo Castle, the Shogun's palace, where the Shoguns lived for 250-odd years until they were obliged to surrender their power to the Meiji Emperor. In certain corridors, the floor is ingeniously constructed so that it squeaks when walked on. No doubt this served its purpose (to warn palace officials and the Shogun himself of approaching assassins), but it must have been quite wearing to live with. The Shogun's quarters (like everyone else, he ate and slept in the same room) were elegantly simple and very sensibly only open to women. We moved on from the castle to the Nishijin quarter, where we wandered about peering into dark little rooms where looms were rattling and Takeshi, not for the first time, got lost.

Lunch next, and Takeshi took me to have *udon*, a kind of soup with noodles and tempura prawns. This was my most difficult meal to date: sitting on the floor with a bowl too hot to pick up and the usual absence of napkins. A good deal of slippery noodles on the trousers. Afterwards, the sun was out and the first stop was the Heian Shrine, the usual orange and green job, but spaciously laid out and extremely imposing. Frustratingly, they were building the stage for the annual ceremonial Noh plays to be performed by firelight over the weekend. I'd love to have seen them. Behind the shrine is a quite wonderful garden with a large lake and irises and

xxvii

white and scarlet water-lilies. Next, up a hill, was the Ginkaku-ji, the Silver Pavilion, so called somewhat preposterously because the Shogun who retired there intended to cover the house with silver, but ultimately didn't. A pretty garden is structured into the lower slopes of one of the mountains with which Kyoto is surrounded – and we had our first sight of a gravel garden, disposed around a strange barrow-like heap, designed to be able (we were told) to hold a dialogue with the moon.

Next stop, as far as I recall, for I was now holding a dialogue with my feet, was the enormous Daitoku-ji complex of temples, in which we first visited the Ryogen-in temple. This contains five small Zen gardens made of gravel, rocks, mosses and small trees: the tiniest one, the Totchiko, is only gravel and rock and is exquisite; the more celebrated Daisen-in near by I was less taken with, such of it as I managed to glimpse through the press.

From here we went to the Kinkaju-ji, the Golden Pavilion. This actually did get round to being covered with gold, but was burnt down by a mad monk (subject of a novel by Mishima) in 1950. The gold on the replica appears to have been specially distressed. The site was intolerably crowded and I was beginning to suffer from cultural indigestion.

However, the next stop was at my request: the Ryoanji, the celebrated Zen garden with fifteen rocks. On the way, the taxi-driver told a no doubt apocryphal story of the Queen's visit to this philosophical monument. Apparently she asked the chief priest what it meant. 'If I explained it to you, you wouldn't understand it,' he replied, 'so why don't you just shut up and look at it? This anecdote seemed to give her (the taxi-driver) a great deal of innocent amusement.

The garden is extraordinarily beautiful, walled in on two sides by a weathered old yellow wall, but so jammed with people it wasn't easy to appreciate. After this, our last stop was the temple overlooking the whole city: Kiyomizu, jumping off which is the proverbial term for a difficult decision. It's approached by a long climb through an arcade of tourist shops, enthusiastically recommended by the taxi-driver, which turned out disappointingly to be the usual agglomeration of garish junk. A swift tramp round the temple: good views, but by now I was longing to get back.

After this, the cedar-wood bath and the dinner were wonderful. However, Takeshi had taken a futher piece of advice from the taxi-driver and booked for us to see geisha dancing at Gion Corner. This turned out to be dire, amateurish and solely designed to part the *gaijin* from his money. The dancing takes up five minutes in a ghastly forty-five minute programme narrated by a solemn American voice, which attempts a crash course in Japanese culture without benefit of either basic staging or talented performers. The tea-ceremony, flower-arranging, playing the thirteen-stringed Koto, a completely unfunny *kyogen* (comic) extract, and a *bunraku* (puppet-theatre) piece with a single puppet all flash past a bewildered audience of plump matrons and perspiring fellows in check trousers.

Back at the hotel, Kichiro calls to tell me he has arranged for me to interview Baroness Ishimoto, an eighty-year-old feminist ex-MP, who sounds like a real-life model for Aiko in the novel. Her only condition is that I read the translation of her autobiography. I agree gratefully.

30 MAY Nine dishes for breakfast today, including seaweed, beans in a kind of whisked egg, a different variety of egg (drinkable) with mushrooms, ladies' fingers and a delicious sort of shredded dried fish with radish. I did a little better this time and then addressed myself to today's problem: John David told me about the all-woman theatre, the Takarazuka, on the outskirts of Osaka and I had asked Takeshi to see if he could get some tickets. He seemed appalled by this idea and this morning told me our only course was to make the 90-minute train journey and hope for the best. To his horror, I agreed to this.

The train left from the basement of the Hankyu department store, which turns out to own the entire Takarazuka complex: a kind of gimcrack Disneyland. At the theatre we learned that the only available tickets were in the gods. Do we want these, Takeshi groaned despairingly; certainly, I said. We then took the monorail which gives you an overview of the whole garish site. The show, *A Tale of Two Cities*, started at one o'clock. Even as we filed in, Takeshi was still frankly incredulous at my insistence on seeing this thing.

The seats were a little cramped but otherwise fine. What ensued was not at all what I'd expected: I'd somehow imagined something progressive, if not feminist. Instead, the show was a cross between panto and operetta, the costumes covered with sparklies, the set frequently changed behind a flimsy curtain with a Dufy-like pattern, while a principal got her teeth into a solo on the forestage or even the cakewalk downstage of the orchestra. There were numerous lavish ensembles (I counted sixty-two women on stage for the trial scene) and a good many memorable moments. The star was Mao Daichi as Sydney Carton (or Sidonie Carton-san, as she was confusingly introduced), who made her smouldering first appearance at a ball in midnight-blue velvet and riding boots. The music was fifties-style ballads emotionally belted out à la Shirley Bassey. There was a jolly tavern number with wenches and a refrain (in English) of 'Thank you very much!'; the French Revolution was represented by a throbbing red spotlight, crowds ebbing and flowing beneath a semi-strobe effect, with music by one of the more excitable Russians; there were balcony scenes and cries of 'Bansai!' from the revolutionaries, giving way to the Marseillaise; and the whole thing whistled by in a brisk ninety minutes. I can see why Takeshi felt I would be wasting my time: on the other hand, this was a good deal more instructive than another day of temples. The audience was especially interesting. If there are 2,500 seats in the theatre, more than 2,000 of them were filled by women: they were having a very good time and out came the occasional discreet hanky as Sidonie declared (left mysteriously alone on an empty stage) that it was a far, far better thing, etc. Why should such an entertainment, inconceivable in England, be so popular? My favourite moment was when a girl in a low-cut dress sank to her knees and said, 'Pierre! Pierre!' exactly like Jean Hagan in *Singin' in the Rain*.

Our next destination was the Hotel Kagetsuan in Hakone, on the slopes of the so far invisible Mt Fuji. It took us five hours to get here (three trains and a taxi), and there was some panic from Takeshi on the final stretch in case we missed dinner (which they apparently stop serving at 8.00). On the bullet train (uncannily punctual as ever), three fourteen-year-old schoolboys came to practise their English on me. They identified themselves as being in the judo club, the basketball club and the kendo club. I gave them some English coins. I was unsure how to divide them, but they played a game and shared the coins according to the result, which seemed good sense. Basketball club told me he had spoken to twenty-four foreigners this year and I was the first Englishman.

The Kagetsuan is a Holiday Inn-style hotel with a hot spring downstairs: Takeshi has just telephoned to exhort me to make use of this. I consulted the hotel information leaflet to check on public bath etiquette, but it doesn't mention the baths. Instead, the first page begins 'HOW TO COPE WITH POTENTIAL DISASTER' and dispenses gloomy advice to do with fire and earthquake. Two pages of this, followed by a perfunctory list of services, including 'sightseeing coarse'. I shall have to make it up as I go along.

I ventured down to the bath in my *yukata* and found it mercifully empty. (I'd been afraid of committing some solecism, such as caused an audible gasp in the dining-room when we got there: I'd forgotten to take my shoes off.) The bath was in a kind of lurid cave, lit from above through a modernist blue, yellow and green stained-glass design, the hot water cascading down into a pool, surrounded by a grey stone area, where you soap and rinse yourself before getting in. The water was buoyant, not too hot, although the whole room is dense with steam; if you sit on the bottom, it covers your shoulders. There's a step, presumably for shorter persons. For some reason, I sneezed a great deal. In the corridor outside, I saw the largest spider I've ever seen outside of captivity. It seemed displeased to meet me and made off like the wind. I returned (bliss!) for a glass of SWEAT from my mini-bar and firmly ordered the Western breakfast for tomorrow.

31 MAY Woke at 5.30: I thought I would look out of the window in the hope of glimpsing Mt Fuji. No sign – just a pretty enough group of wooded hills across a lake. So when I got up at 7.00 and had another look, first glancing at the lake and then letting my eyes drift to the right, I literally gasped to see the familiar contours of the black volcanic slopes and snowy crown. I took a picture of it fast, before it should take it into its head to disappear again.

I breakfasted in solitary splendour in the Western restaurant and have seldom been so pleased to see the humble cornflake. Half-way through, Takeshi joined me, having bolted his eight courses across the way, and worked through his usual repertoire: slurps (he'd ordered coffee), grunts of satisfaction, gargling sighs and constant lighting of his Hope cigarettes. He seemed quite particularly harassed, his expression that of a man compelled to superintend a potentially troublesome lunatic. I, on my side, was preoccupied with a simple question: why were we here? Was this the rump or vestige of the 'script conference' referred to when the visit to Hakone was first mooted? I decided the trick would be to get back to Tokyo as soon as possible.

This hotel, in which we appear to be the only guests, is a rum sort of place. Loud Bavarian-style muzak in all public areas (except the baths) and, astonishingly, hanging on the landing of what is probably called the mezzanine, a Gainsborough: two ladies and a child on a donkey. Who would be more astonished: Gainsborough, here, or Dickens if you sat him down in front of the Takarazuka?

Later, back in Tokyo: after what seemed like paroxysms of indecision, Takeshi summoned a driver and we set off round the Hakone area. There was more than a whiff of sulphur in the air and the first stop was a cable-car station near a series of fissures in the mountains, from which steam rose from pools of bright yellow bubbling sulphur. We took the cable-car down to Lake Hakone and embarked upon a gaudily painted red, blue and gilt 'pirate ship' called the 'Captain Kidd' for a cruise across the lake, which lasted an hour or so. This was very enjoyable, although it was difficult to imagine what light it might throw on the experiences of a Scotswoman in Japan during the Meiji era. Mt Fuji was spectacularly visible throughout. We then visited the inevitable shrine of three, artfully hidden in the pine woods and had lunch at a Western-style restaurant kitted out inside like a ship; the decor, however, compensated for by a sensational view across the lake. As I ate (some sort of local whitebait) Fuji-san drew his clouds around him and vanished for an afternoon nap. He was scarcely visible again, but I'm told I was extremely lucky to see so much of the mountain so clearly.

We set off again along the scenic route, the driver delivering us to all the local sights. Finally, after a long traipse through a large but understocked botanical garden, I told Takeshi it was essential for me to return to Tokyo and the driver dropped us off at Odawara station. Back in Tokyo, we bought my ticket to Karuizawa, a mysterious about-face having occurred. Last week, Takeshi, trying to dissuade me from going to Karuizawa, said it was impossible to get there and back in a single day. Now, when I wondered which hotel I should stay at, he put on a show of amazement. Hotel? What hotel? It was quite unnecessary to take a hotel, when to return to Tokyo was so simple and convenient. Poor Takeshi must have been delighted to drop me off at the hotel: I seem not to have made life very easy for him. My abiding image for the trip is Takeshi, at the Takarazuka theatre, standing under a huge sign marked 'Information' in several languages, his expression woebegone, his back to an efficient-looking uniformed girl behind the desk, appealing to me urgently: 'But who shall we ask?'

1 JUNE My trip to Karuizawa could scarcely have been simpler. I took the subway to Veno; the train to Karuizawa; a taxi to the Prince Hotel (selected at random); I spoke to a young man; he fetched a young woman; I presented my card (a bilingual affair, run up for me by JAL); I explained my requirements; she went off to consult and returned saying the manager was not inclined to let me take photographs in the hotel grounds; I told her this was perfectly fine and not my intention, I just needed someone (her) to find me a taxi-driver and explain what I wanted; she came back with a bright young driver and helped us to negotiate a deal; we drove around; I found and photographed old hotels, old private houses, old tennis courts, all amid pine forests, very beautiful, eminently filmable; he took me back to the station. I was back at the hotel by 8.00.

The approaches to Karuizawa are guarded by high, wooded hills with sheer drops and summits of a fantastical shape, rather like those in Chinese paintings. The town itself affects a kind of Swiss atmosphere (complete with electronic cuckoo-clock: hence perhaps the term 'Japanese Alps'). The train was full of exuberant weekenders with tennis racquets or golf-clubs. I only experienced one moment of bewilderment: when the packed lunch I'd adventurously bought at the station seemed to have no chopsticks. (Should they have been bought separately? Does one bring one's own? What to do?) Eventually I discovered them neatly taped (together with the statutory toothpick) to the side of the box.

The Karuizawa scenes were eventually shot at Kurashiki.

2 JUNE Naonori collected me from the hotel, drove me out to his charming apartment, where he lives with his wife and children (girl of thirteen, boy of ten), took me for a stroll in his local park (which has a racetrack, show-jumping course and riding school) and provided the best Indian tea (which I showed them how to make, according to my granny's formula). At 4.30, curry was

served. I had said to Takeshi that if Naonori's invitation was for lunch, I would go to the 6.30 performance of *Ran*; if for dinner, the 2.30 performance. Clearly, some misunderstanding had occurred, for during the meal Naonori mildly remarked that this was an unusually early hour for dinner in Japan, but that since I had an early evening ticket for *Ran* . . . At the conclusion of the meal, the little boy presented me with one of his comics for my children and Mrs Kawamura gave me some Japanese crackers for the plane. I responded with my last piece of Harrods' Wedgwood and one or two gifts of my own. A ceremonial photograph was taken in the car park, then Naonori drove me to the cinema. On the way he revealed that the Chinese had agreed to let us film in China.

See note above re. Manchuria.

Naonori had told me that *Ran* was not highly thought of at NHK and clearly the Japanese audience were not specially taken with it, judging by the amount of chatter, coughing, yawning, snoring and wandering in and out which went on. Nevertheless, I loved it: it looks magnificent, filmed largely on plains of black volcanic ash on the slopes of Mt Fuji; and the use of the Lear material is, of course, fascinating. Lear has sons rather than daughters (this reminded me of the Japanese equivalent of chess, *shogi*, which Naonori showed me this afternoon. It has twenty pieces on each side and a board of nine squares by nine, but when I asked which piece was the queen, Naonori was surprised. 'This is a soldiers' game', he said, 'there is no queen.'), which makes historical sense, but robs the final reconciliation scene with the youngest child of the unbearable pathos of Shakespeare.

Daisuke Ryu, our Kurihama-to-be, played the Cordelia part in Ran.

The battle sequences are an object lesson (the five separate armies helpfully colour-coded) and the first and best of them is played without sound-effects (except for the grave and melancholy music) until the single musket-shot which kills the eldest son. A Goneril-like character (widow of the eldest son) marries the second son, who is the principal villain, reminiscent of Macbeth. In the storm scene, the hut they find is not Edgar's (there is no Gloucester figure), but belongs to a boy Lear has had blinded as a child, the brother of his second son's first wife. The young actor playing the Fool I recognized from a TV chat show I'd been watching last week, on which he'd appeared in rather arresting drag, sequinned miniskirt and giant earrings; his role was central, his jokes rather different in timbre from Shakespeare's ('Man is born crying,' he says at one point, 'and when he has cried enough, he dies.'). Lear looks like Robert Helpmann as Don Quixote. The final image (after tremendous slaughter) has the blind man, alone on a cliff-edge, having dropped his protective picture of Buddha, completely abandoned. I was dispirited that the local audience seemed so unimpressed.

3 JUNE I reported to NHK to see Ken Miyamoto. It had been announced that we were going to his home, but I realized this would not be the case when he presented me, in the foyer of NHK with a copy of *Total Eclipse* in Japanese and two presents – one for us (a tablecloth) and another for Arnold and Dusty. We went to a nearby restaurant, where I interviewed him for two hours. Then I asked him if he had any questions. He immediately began to speak of the final scene of the film, discussing its possibilities and ambiguities, finally settling on the question of Ozaki's rank. This had already been exhaustively discussed at the script conference, to my surprise, since it seemed a matter of singular unimportance; later, I concluded that what was difficult for them to accept was that a man with non-Japanese blood could achieve advancement in the army. Eventually, I told Ken I was quite happy to demote Ozaki to Captain. All was saved! General satisfaction. Handshakes.

The afternoon interview was with Professor Shinzo Ogi, NHK's official historian, a small gentleman with a courtly manner who tended to give enormous answers to simple questions, answers bristling with so many dates that Sam was hard pressed to cope. I gleaned some useful facts on specific points and, at 6.30, made my way back to the hotel in the gathering darkness.

I paid a farewell visit to my local sushi bar, where the atmosphere is pleasantly informal (on my first visit they wanted to switch the TV off for my benefit, but I wouldn't let them). I pointed to my selection (tonight I was the only customer) and, rising above a mishap involving soy sauce and white trousers, had a delicious meal and a flask of sake for £3. Now I must pack and finish the Baroness's book.

4 JUNE I left the Tokyo City Air Terminal five hours before my flight: a little on the cautious side, but in truth there was nothing more for me to do in Tokyo. The airport bus was a mere £8.50, compared to the £70-odd you would expect to pay for a taxi, was extremely comfortable and got here (the airport) in an hour, starting along that expressway which gives you an overhead view of the city not unlike early sequences in *Blade Runner*, surely the most haphazard jumble in urban history. It was starting to rain and an iron-grey sky sat on a thin blue line above a pinky-orange pollution haze. On we go, past hundreds of high-rise flats, flexibly anchored, I hope, against earthquake, past the Queen Elizabeth Love Hotel (shaped like a ship), the 10 hotel, a vast 10-pin bowling hall and a monster Pachinko Playland Parlour. Then across a small river clogged with foamy effluent, past a valley of rice fields, in which the sun, making a rare farewell appearance, was vividly reflected, and out into the rural areas. I missed the towers and minarets, the dreaming spires of the Tokyo Disneyland, which had surprised me on the way in. Once in the airport I made the fatal mistake of passing too swiftly through customs and found myself in a bleak corridor with a few backless chairs and a comfortable-looking bar hovering tantalizingly (and now inaccessibly) one floor above. There was nothing for it but to press on to the circular capsule from which the planes actually leave, where an armchair came free when the flight to Honolulu was called. So here I am for the next three hours.

Naonori arrived early at the hotel to say goodbye and present me with a very pretty little lacquered wine-glass. I returned the famous NHK ice-blue umbrella and he went off with it, garishly incongruous against his sober suit.

Takeshi and Sam then took me off to meet the Baroness, which I'm afraid was something of a disappointment. She was prepared to talk only in polite chichés, interspersed with a stern warning not to use anything from her book and an eloquent plea to Takeshi to buy the rights and serialize it. She spoke English and once she'd misunderstood my first question (which was whether the pre-First World War period is as idyllically nostalgic for the Japanese as it is for the British) and answered with a lengthy diatribe against the

xxxvi

inadequacies and delinquencies of today's youth, I'm afraid I more or less gave up. It was fascinating to meet her and I hope I have as many marbles when I'm eighty-eight, but the book was much more useful than the meeting. After an hour and a half and a lengthy paean of praise for Mrs Thatcher, I made our excuses and left.

Lunch with Takeshi and Sam. I requested tempura and they took me to a very handsome restaurant; in its large fish-tank, however, a fish was floating disconcertingly belly-up.

Our final interview was with Mr Sadaichi Ichihashi, retired head of department from the Matsuzakaya department store: it turned out to be probably the most useful of the entire trip. A dapper, twinkling party, looking far younger than seventy-two, despite the white streaks in his hair, he had prepared helpful notes about the *modus operandi* of the store (which he had joined in 1931) and brought with him two bound volumes of the Matsuzakaya house magazine. These were wrapped in his *furoshiki* (a kind of reversible bandana, with a serious colour for tragic occasions and a lighter colour, now outermost, for happy occasions, the owner's name elegantly stitched in one corner). He answered all my questions, volunteered a good many useful pieces of information and was generally a model interviewee and, it seemed to me, a contented man.

After this, I said goodbye to Sam and took a taxi with Takeshi (who today seemed markedly more cheerful) to the Terminal. His final injunction as we parted was a request for a good script.

Christopher Hampton

The Ginger Tree was first transmitted on BBC TV in November 1989, in four episodes.

The cast included:

MARY	Samantha Bond
RICHARD	Adrian Rawlins
ALICIA	Joanna McCallum
ISABELLE	Cécile Paoli
ARMAND	Jean Badin
BOB DALE	Colin Stinton
EMMA LOU DALE	Barbara Barnes
KENTARO	Daisuke Ryu
AIKO	Fumi Dan

Director	Tony Garner
Producer	Tim Ironside-Wood
Executive Producer	Alan Shallcross
Associate Producer	Nick Hawkins
Script Editor	Colin Ludlow
Costume Designer	Michael Burdle

For NHK, Japan

Director	Morimasa Matsumoto
Executive Producer	Naonori Kawamura
Designer	Hiromi Saito
Costume	Keiji Iwasaki

ONE

EXT. MANDARIN'S PALACE IN MUKDEN. DAY
*The palace, set in a commanding position at the top of a low hill, is
one of a group of small mansions forming satellites to the grandiose
but abandoned Imperial Palace, the walls of which can be glimpsed
in the background. The impression is of a baroque riot of red roofs
and Chinese gargoyles spreading away into the distance.
The camera contemplates the house from within the large walled
courtyard in front of it. A droshky waits, decorated with flowers and
white ribbon, its Chinese driver looking uncomfortable in morning-
coat and top-hat.
A bright summer's day.
A caption: 'Mukden, Manchuria, 1903'.*

INT. MARY MACKENZIE'S DRESSING-ROOM. MANDARIN'S
PALACE. DAY
MARY MACKENZIE *is a fresh-faced Scotswoman of about twenty,
with a candid and inquisitive expression, whose voice has the lilt of
a light Morningside accent. She's wearing a high-necked white silk
wedding dress. Kneeling beside her on the floor is a seamstress, a
little old Chinese woman with a mouthful of pins, who is diligently
working on the dress's lace trimming. At a certain moment the
seamstress looks up and smiles warmly at* MARY
MARY *returns the smile, moved. Then her eye strays to her dressing-
table, on which there stands the framed photograph of an extremely
handsome young man in army uniform:* RICHARD
COLLINGSWORTH. MARY *contemplates the photograph, her
expression solemn.*

EXT. MANOR HOUSE IN THE HIGHLANDS. DAY. 1902
MARY *stands with her friend* MARGARET BLAIR, *at the back of the
house belonging to Margaret's parents, watching as a horse and rider
gallop across the fields behind the house, jump the fence with some
brio and thunder towards them.
As the horse approaches it becomes clear that the rider is* RICHARD.
He's wearing his army uniform. He reins in close to where the girls

I

are standing and dismounts with a flourish. MARGARET, *a plain but lively young woman, calls over to him.*

MARGARET: What have you done with my brother, Mr Collingsworth?

RICHARD: I'm afraid he's far too cautious for me, Miss Blair. I'm addicted to danger.

(MARY *is watching him with obvious approval.*)

EXT. CROQUET LAWN. DAY. 1902
RICHARD *and* MARY, *partners in the croquet match against* MARGARET *and her brother, are somewhat behind the others, waiting their turn.*

MARY: How long will you be in Hong Kong?

RICHARD: It's a five-year tour of duty. But Hong Kong is only my base. From there I have to be prepared to go wherever the Chief of Staff may decide to send me.

MARY: I can't imagine it. Coming up here to stay with Margaret is the furthest I've ever travelled from Edinburgh.

RICHARD: Perhaps I can tempt you to take a trip abroad.

MARY: What do you mean?

(*She blushes, looking at him in alarm.*)

RICHARD: Only that I thought you might enjoy spending a few days at my family's estate in Norfolk.

MARY: Oh, I see.

(*It's* MARY *and* RICHARD'*s turn to play. Quite calmly and deliberately but out of sight of the opposition,* RICHARD *adjusts the position of his ball to a more advantageous spot and whacks it resoundingly through the hoop. Then he winks at* MARY.)

RICHARD: That's better.

(*He sets off down the lawn, with* MARY *following.*)

I'll write to your mother and invite you, if I may.

INT. MARY'S DRESSING-ROOM. MANDARIN'S PALACE. DAY
The seamstress is just finishing off her task when the door opens and an elegant woman of about twenty-seven, with an impressively cool and authoritative manner, walks into the room, expensively and fashionably dressed for her role of matron of honour.
This is ISABELLE DE CHAMONPIERRE, *whose English is very good, while still unmistakably identifying her as French.*

ISABELLE: Are you ready?

2

MARY: Almost.

ISABELLE: After to have made such an epic journey to reach us here, there would be no logic to be late at the church, don't you think?

(MARY *smiles at her, remembering.*)

EXT. DECK OF THE SS CHING WHA. VLADIVOSTOCK HARBOUR. DAY

March 1903. The SS Ching Wha, *a battered coal-ship, has just docked.*

MARY *is standing in a corner of the deck, her eyes fixed on the harbour, inadequately protected against the cold, but unable to tear herself away from the spectacle.*

Nearby, a packed group of drably dressed Chinese passengers are slowly beginning to disembark.

Her attention divided between the Chinese and the harbour, MARY *doesn't notice the arrival of a young Jesuit in a black robe,* FATHER ANTHONY, *who comes to stand next to her at the rail, startling her when he eventually speaks.*

ANTHONY: Imagine what it must be like in winter. I'll be glad to get out of Russia.

(MARY *nods, smiling, clearly excited by the prospect of arrival.*)

MARY: The first officer said it was very dangerous, where you're going.

ANTHONY: Not really. It was, during the Boxer Rising, but that's all over now.

MARY: He said they did terrible things.

ANTHONY: Yes. In Shansi province everyone in our mission was killed and their heads displayed on pikes.

MARY: Aren't you frightened?

(FATHER ANTHONY *doesn't answer for a moment, he looks at her shrewdly.*)

ANTHONY: The man you've come out here to marry, Mr . . .

MARY: Collingsworth.

ANTHONY: How many times have you met him?

(MARY *frowns, puzzled.*)

MARY: Twice in Scotland and then I spent a weekend with his family in Norfolk. Why?

ANTHONY: I've put myself in God's hands. Whatever may

3

happen, I know I have nothing to fear. But if I were on my way to spend my life with someone I'd only met three times, I might really be frightened.
(MARY *looks away, troubled.*)

EXT. LOWER DECK OF THE SS CHING WHA. DAY
MARY *moves expectantly towards the head of the gangplank as a man in a fur hat and coat,* MICHAEL EVANS, *makes his way through the disembarking passengers to greet her.*
EVANS: Miss Mackenzie?
MARY: That's right.
EVANS: Not the best news, I'm afraid. Last week your fiancé was ordered south to Russian GHQ in Manchuria.
MARY: He's not here?
EVANS: I'm Evans, Michael Evans. I have a coal mine just outside the city.
(MARY *shakes hands with him, a little stiffly.*)
If you wouldn't mind waiting a moment, I have some coolies arriving. I'd best go and sort them out.
MARY: Of course.
(EVANS *turns away, then back again, slipping off his coat.*)
EVANS: You'd better have this.
(*He wraps it around* MARY, *who practically vanishes inside it, and hurries off.*
In the background, FATHER ANTHONY *has been greeted by his colleagues and is now being escorted by them to the gangplank.*
He turns to wave to MARY *and she waves back, shaking her head to convey to him what has happened.*
He looks concerned, but the other Jesuits are hurrying him away.)

INT. LIVING-ROOM IN MICHAEL EVANS'S HOUSE. EVENING
MARY *sits alone, huddled against the stove in a large, gloomy, ill-lit room with pine floors.*
Presently EVANS *appears with two oil-lamps, which he places at either end of a long table.*
EVANS: I know how you must feel, but I don't see what alternative there is to your taking the boat back to Hong Kong when it leaves at the end of the week.
MARY: Is that what Richard wanted?

4

EVANS: To tell you the truth, he wasn't best pleased to hear
you'd set off in the first place. He said if there'd been time,
he would have stopped you. There's nothing up here, as
you can see.

MARY: But how long is he going to be in Manchuria?

EVANS: I don't know, not more than a few months, a year at
most.

MARY: A year!

INT. BEDROOM. NIGHT
Moonlight streams into the uncurtained spare bedroom which MARY
has been given. Outside the wind is howling.
MARY's *eyes are wide open. She sits up and reaches for her*
handbag, which is on the chair by her bed. She opens the bag, takes
an envelope out of it and reassures herself as to its contents, a
number of large, white, flimsy five-pound notes, quite identifiable in
the moonlight.

INT. LIVING-ROOM. DAY
EVANS *has almost finished his breakfast.* MARY *sips from a glass of*
tea. The samovar bubbles on the stove.

MARY: Couldn't I just go to the station and buy a ticket?
(EVANS *looks up. Though still polite, he is clearly becoming a*
little exasperated with MARY.)

EVANS: They don't sell tickets. Most of the way it's only a
goods route *and* you're not allowed to travel without a
permit *and* they'd never give you one. Even if they did, it's
a week's journey and you'd have to change at Nokolsk and
Grodikov and Pogranitsa, at any of which you might have
to wait days. And on top of that, it's extremely dangerous
country. A woman travelling alone, it'd be suicide. I really
can't allow it.

MARY: Supposing I could find an escort?
(EVANS *sighs, then frowns at her as a thought occurs to him.*)

EVANS: I couldn't get away, if that's what you're thinking.

MARY: That's not what I'm thinking.

EXT. QUADRANGLE. CATHOLIC CHURCH. DAY
As MARY *enters the quadrangle,* FATHER ANTHONY *emerges from a*

5

makeshift cloister at right-angles to her. He looks up sharply,
surprised but not displeased to see her.
ANTHONY: Why, Miss Mackenzie!
    (MARY *advances towards him.*)
MARY: How soon are you leaving for Manchuria?

EXT. VLADIVOSTOCK STATION. NIGHT
MARY *and* FATHER ANTHONY *wait to board the train, a*
ramshackle collection of battered carriages, very few of them with
compartments. Most of the passengers are Chinese.
MICHAEL EVANS *hurries up to them, carrying a carpet-bag and a*
bundle under his arm.
EVANS: Brought you a few supplies. You'll get no food on this
    journey.
    (*He hands her the carpet-bag and unfurls his bundle, which*
    turns out to be a rough sleeveless overcoat, wool on the inside,
    sheepskin outside.)
    Doesn't smell too good, but it'll keep you warm.
MARY: I don't know if I can accept . . .
EVANS: Nonsense, they practically give them away.
    (MARY *takes the coat.*)
MARY: Well, thank you, you've been very kind.
EVANS: Give my regards to Collingsworth. He's a lucky man.
    (*He looks away, embarrassed.*)

EXT. BORDER STATION. EVENING
MARY *and* FATHER ANTHONY *join the crowds descending from the*
train, which has now reached its terminus.
The station consists of a long wooden barn-like structure with
occasional suspended oil-lamps. At intervals along the platform,
which consists of bare earth, there are crackling open wood-fires,
around which knots of exhausted passengers gather. It's raining
heavily. There are a great many armed Russian soldiers walking
around.
ANTHONY: I'll go and find out when the next train leaves.
    (MARY *nods and as he heads off, she finds a sheltered spot not*
    far from one of the fires and sits down on her bag.
    After a time, a man in a sheepskin coat identical to hers looms
    over her and offers her some blackened meat on a kebab. MARY

6

begins fumbling for her purse and he shakes his head and hands
her the kebab. She smiles and he bows and leaves. MARY *tests*
the kebab gingerly; it turns out to be delicious. She's
demolishing it, when FATHER ANTHONY *reappears, his*
expression woebegone.)
Tomorrow afternoon.

EXT. RAILWAY LINE. NIGHT
A long goods-train rattles across bleak plains.

INT. CATTLE TRUCK. NIGHT
MARY *is lying on straw amid rolls of telegraph wire, using her bag*
as a pillow. She wakes as the train shudders to a halt.

EXT. RAILWAY LINE. NIGHT
It's a clear cold night. The sky is full of stars. The train has stopped,
presumably for some time, as fires have been built alongside the
train. Someone is playing a concertina.

INT./EXT. CATTLE TRUCK. NIGHT
FATHER ANTHONY *is asleep.*
MARY *stands in the doorway, looking out across the vast plain.*
Down the line, the concertina is joined by a single deep voice,
singing a melancholy Cossack refrain. MARY *shivers and picks a*
piece of straw from her hair.

EXT. MANDARIN'S PALACE IN MUKDEN. DAY
MARY, *resplendent in her wedding dress, veiled, climbs into the*
droshky, followed by ISABELLE DE CHAMONPIERRE. *The driver*
flicks his whip languidly at the horses. MARY'S *eyes shine brightly*
through her veil.

INT./EXT. TRAIN COMPARTMENT. DAY
MARY *and* FATHER ANTHONY *are once again in a train*
compartment. Now all the other passengers are Chinese.
Outside there has been a total transformation in the landscape,
which is lush, rolling terrain, woods and grass and millet-fields, not
in any way typically Oriental, except for the occasional Chinese-style

buildings. There are magpies in the trees and the bright greens and
wild flowers of spring.
MARY *has opened a tin of ham from the carpet-bag. She hacks off a*
chunk and hands it to FATHER ANTHONY.
MARY: This is more like it, isn't it?
ANTHONY: Yes, it's rather like Sussex.
> (*At this point, the train suddenly brakes joltingly going round a*
> *curve and grinds to a standstill.* MARY's *window is close to a*
> *telegraph pole. Suspended from the arms of the pole are three*
> *open-sided wooden boxes. Each of them contains a head,*
> *discernibly Chinese in features, one with a pigtail hanging*
> *down out of the box.*
> MARY *and* ANTHONY *contemplate this for a moment,*
> *appalled, and then turn to face each other.*)
MARY: Well, not altogether like Sussex.

EXT. STREETS OF MUKDEN. DAY
The droshky picks its way delicately through the crowded streets.
MARY *is lost in thought.* ISABELLE *leans across to her.*
ISABELLE: What are you thinking about?
> (MARY *hesitates, then points across the road at a broad gate.*)
MARY: The day I arrived in Mukden.
> (*The gate is the entrance to the Dragon Inn.*)

EXT. STREETS OF MUKDEN. DAY
March 1903. MARY *is now travelling in the opposite direction. She*
is alone in another droshky, in her travel-stained clothes, carpet-bag
on her knee. The droshky turns through a gate into:

EXT. DRAGON INN. DAY
The courtyard of the Der-Lung-Djen or Dragon Inn. This consists of
a number of one-storey houses arranged around a central compound
(*the courtyard*), *which is used among other things for the stabling of*
horses.
MARY *climbs down from her droshky, as does the driver, who ties up*
the horses and vanishes in the direction of the hotel owner's house,
leaving MARY *waiting by the droshky. There are a few people,*
moving to and fro across the broad courtyard; among them, MARY
suddenly notices a young officer in the process, with the help of two
Chinese servants, of saddling his horse. MARY, *once her attention is*

8

caught, peers across at him. Eventually MARY *sets off across the courtyard towards the young officer, moving more quickly as she realizes the young man really is* RICHARD.

MARY *calls to* RICHARD *before he becomes aware of her presence.*

MARY: Richard!

(*He turns to look at her, surprised. For a moment, it's quite clear that he fails to recognize her. Then, when he does, he looks far from pleased to see her.*)

RICHARD: Mary?

MARY: Yes.

RICHARD: What on earth are you doing here?

MARY: Well . . .

(*Her face falls at his obvious lack of enthusiasm.*)

RICHARD: I told Evans to send you back to Hong Kong.

MARY: I didn't want to go.

RICHARD: But this is no place for a woman.

MARY: I saw quite a lot of women on my way here from the station.

RICHARD: You know perfectly well what I mean.

MARY: So . . . aren't you pleased to see me?

RICHARD: Of course I am, it's just . . . for one thing, where are you going to stay?

MARY: Well, here, I suppose.

RICHARD: I can't allow you to stay in the same hotel, not before we're married, it wouldn't be right.

MARY: I don't see the harm in it.

RICHARD: I'm surprised at you!

(MARY *bows her head, miserably. Then* RICHARD, *finally aware that it's incumbent on him to make some sort of gesture, steps over to her and pinions her briefly in a perfunctory embrace. She clings on to him for a moment and he kisses her cheek.* RICHARD *stands back to look at her disapprovingly.*)

What are you wearing?

INT. RUSSIAN RESTAURANT. EVENING

MARY *sits opposite* RICHARD, *wearing a slightly crumpled but still elegant evening gown.* RICHARD *himself is in evening dress. The restaurant's glass and dark wood art nouveau furnishings are a spirited imitation of* Maxim's *in Paris. It's crowded with a more or*

*less exclusively Russian clientele, who are greatly enjoying the small
balalaika orchestra: three musicians in red blouses and navy-blue
zouaves.*

MARY: Can't I stay at the inn?

RICHARD: No, I'm sure you'll be far more comfortable with the
de Chamonpierres. And it'll be a relief to me to know
you're being properly looked after.

MARY: What's she doing here? I thought you said this was no
place for a woman.

RICHARD: Well, you know the French, they have quite
different ideas. And in their case, a good fat private income
to back them up. I can't say he's much of a soldier. Always
slipping away to pick flowers when he's supposed to be
watching manoeuvres.

MARY: It's kind of them.

RICHARD: They have half-a-dozen servants, it won't be the
slightest trouble.

MARY: I hope it won't be for too long.

RICHARD: As long as it takes me to find a church, set a date and
locate a house I can afford. They see you coming, these
people, think of a number and double it.
(*He falls silent for a moment: then, abruptly, he reaches into his
pocket, takes out a small box and pushes it across to* MARY,
who has just finished her pheasant. MARY *opens the box. It
contains an amethyst engagement ring, set in seed pearls.* MARY
takes it out and holds it up to the candlelight.)

MARY: It's lovely.

RICHARD: Korean amethyst. Try it on.
(MARY *slips the ring on to her ring finger. It's a perfect fit.*)
You see. I remembered the exact size.

MARY: You got Mama to send you the measurement.

RICHARD: I had it made in Hong Kong. Bunch of thieves, but
the workmanship is very fine.
(MARY *is aware of the gracelessness of this remark;
nevertheless, she smiles gratefully.*)

MARY: Thank you, Richard.
(*The orchestra begins to play, in its own melancholy and
eccentric Slavonic style, 'Danny Boy'.* MARY *turns,
remembering.*)

EXT. MACKENZIE HOUSE IN EDINBURGH. EVENING. 1902
'Danny Boy' again, but this time, in the distance, in MARY's *pure soprano, accompanied at the piano.*
It's dusk. A couple of carriages stand in the driveway of a substantial Morningside property. The breath of the horses rises on the cold evening air.

INT. MACKENZIE HOUSE IN EDINBURGH. EVENING.
The camera tracks through the hallway and the dark front parlour to the brightly lit drawing-room, the sound of 'Danny Boy' increasing as we approach.
In the drawing-room MARY *stands by the piano, singing, accompanied by a young friend. As the song draws to a close,* MARY *smiles in the direction of the audience, a dozen or so formally dressed, mostly young people, including* RICHARD, *impeccable in his dress uniform. Next to him is Mary's mother, benevolently beating time with her fan.*
MARY's *point of view: Mrs Mackenzie leans over to murmur something to* RICHARD, *who responds earnestly. He goes on talking to her behind her fan, his expression intent and shrewd, only breaking off to applaud enthusiastically when* MARY *finishes the song.*

EXT. DROSHKY. DAY
ISABELLE DE CHAMONPIERRE *leans over to murmur into* MARY's *ear.*
ISABELLE: How is it, to be about to marry the most beautiful young man in Mukden?
MARY: Is that what you think?
ISABELLE: Oh, yes, he is very good decoration. That's why I like so much to have him at my table.

INT. DINING-ROOM IN THE MANDARIN'S PALACE. NIGHT
RICHARD *looks up sharply from his position at the centre of the long mahogany table in the lavish dining-room. It is* ISABELLE DE CHAMONPIERRE *and her husband,* ARMAND, *a handsome, mild-looking man of about forty, slightly vague and scholarly in manner, who are the hosts of the dinner party in their rented palace, and they sit at either end of the table.* MARY, *the only female guest, is seated*

11

on ARMAND's *right. The other guests are almost all young men in uniform, not too many for the conversation to become general from time to time when so orchestrated by* ISABELLE.

RICHARD: But you see, Madame, the Russians simply must have an ice-free harbour in the winter.

ISABELLE: And you believe this justifies their transparent manoeuvrings in Korea, do you?
(The focus shifts to ARMAND, *who leans over to murmur to* MARY.)

ARMAND: I'm sure you have already understood that my wife has much better knowledge of military and political realities than I.

MARY: Yes, I'm afraid I have no idea at all what's going on.

ARMAND: Well, nothing. I can't tell you what a boring winter it has been. Everyone is making belligerent noises but always they back off at the last moment. In any case, I must confess, my real enthusiasm is for botany, but even this is impossible when the whole country is for months under snow and ice . . .
*(*ISABELLE's *voice is now raised in dispute with* RICHARD.)

ISABELLE: And I tell you that the Russians are behaving with unforgivable arrogance.

RICHARD: Perhaps you're right, Madame. All I'm saying is for the Japanese to declare war on them would be absolutely suicidal.

VOICE: (Off-screen) Suicide is not considered a disgrace in my country, the way it seems to be in the West. In certain conditions, we believe it can be the noblest course.
(The speaker, who now comes into view, has unexpectedly captured the attention of the table. He is COUNT KENTARO KURIHAMA, *an impressive-looking black-uniformed Japanese of about thirty, still and contained.*
RICHARD *is more than a little startled by his intervention.)*

RICHARD: Not very constructive though, is it?

KENTARO: It's a question of attitude. Our history is full of examples of suicidal gestures which have transformed the pattern of events.
(A slight pause is filled by ISABELLE, *efficiently fulfilling her role as hostess.)*

ISABELLE: Myself, I have always said, one Japanese soldier is
    worth three Russians.
RICHARD: He could be worth five and still be outnumbered.
KENTARO: We feel there are more important considerations
    than numbers.
    (*As the conversation becomes general again,* ARMAND *leans
    across to* MARY.)
ARMAND: Technically, of course, my government supports the
    Russians in this dispute, but Isabelle knows she is among
    friends.
MARY: Who is that gentleman?
ARMAND: He is the Japanese equivalent of Richard or myself,
    the Military Attaché, Count Kentaro Kurihama. He was a
    great hero in the Siege of Peking.
    (MARY *looks up the table to find that* KENTARO, *his expression
    remote, is staring at her. She looks away, confused.*)

EXT. DROSHKY. DAY
By now, the droshky is on its final approaches to the church. MARY
turns to ISABELLE, *afflicted by some last-minute feeling of
insecurity.*
MARY: I suppose you must wonder what Richard ever saw in
    me.
ISABELLE: No, no; I'm sure there is some very logical
    arrangement.
MARY: Arrangement!
ISABELLE: Oh, forgive me, sometimes my English . . .
MARY: Your English is excellent.
    (ISABELLE *considers her levelly for a moment.*)
ISABELLE: Why do you suppose peope always want to cry at
    weddings?

EXT. UNITED FREE CHURCH OF SCOTLAND. DAY
*The droshky draws up at the church, which is red brick and
functional, a weird architectural interruption of the otherwise
warren-like Oriental street. Outside the church are several other
droshkys and their drivers, numbers of tethered horses and a
scattering of rickshaws.*
MARY *and* ISABELLE *descend and move towards the church door.*

13

INT. CHURCH. DAY
Inside the plain brick and wood church, the congregation is
predominantly male and European.
ARMAND DE CHAMONPIERRE *takes* MARY's *arm, and, as the*
'Lohengrin' march begins, leads her down the aisle.
MARY's *point of view:* RICHARD *turns to watch her approach.*
KENTARO *is in the congregation: for some reason* MARY *is drawn to*
look at him, but he's staring straight ahead.
RICHARD *waits, below the plain altar.*

EXT. MANOR HOUSE IN THE HIGHLANDS. DAY
As before, RICHARD *reins in his horse and dismounts.*

INT. CHURCH. DAY
MARY *speaks the responses in a firm, clear voice.*

EXT. CHURCH. DAY
From inside the building comes the rousing sound of the hymn:
'Praise my Soul, the King of Heaven'.

INT. CHURCH. DAY
As the hymn continues, RICHARD *and* MARY *proceed down the*
aisle.
This time, KENTARO *is staring directly at* MARY, *now unveiled. As*
she passes, she meets his gaze and smiles at him. He stares back at
her, impassive.

EXT. STREET. DAY
RICHARD *and* MARY *sit arm-in-arm in the droshky, which is*
travelling quite fast down one of the broader streets in the Walled
City. The droshky turns into one of the quieter side-streets, deserted
except for the old seamstress, who appears to be waiting for them. As
the droshky approaches she shuffles forward and bows deeply. MARY
turns to look back at her as she rises, smiling toothlessly. MARY
smiles back, evidently moved.

EXT. MANDARIN'S PALACE. DAY
RICHARD *has* MARY's *arm, he leads her in the front door of the*
palace.

INT. ENTRANCE HALL IN THE MANDARIN'S PALACE. DAY
As RICHARD *hands his hat and gloves to a servant, he notices a*
spectacular tricorne hat with ostrich-feather plumes.
RICHARD: Ah, Sir Claude *has* come.

INT. DRAWING-ROOM IN THE MANDARIN'S PALACE. DAY
As RICHARD *and* MARY *enter the principal salon to a polite ripple*
of applause, they encounter, just inside the door, KENTARO
KURIHAMA, *who is talking to a tall, distinguished-looking man*
with substantial waxed moustaches: SIR CLAUDE MACDONALD,
the British Minister, in full Imperial regalia. He addresses them in a
crisp Scottish accent.
SIR CLAUDE: Ah, the happy couple.
KENTARO: Have you met Sir Claude MacDonald?
MARY: No.
  (*She shakes hands with him, as does* RICHARD.)
RICHARD: This is a very great honour.
SIR CLAUDE: Not at all, I'm delighted I happened to be up
  here. Always enjoy a wedding.
  (*There's a minute's awkward silence and then* SIR CLAUDE
  exercises his diplomatic skills.)
  I was just explaining to our friend here, I've been posted
  Ambassador to Tokyo.
RICHARD: I didn't know that.
SIR CLAUDE: I'm delighted, of course. I've always been a great
  admirer of the Japanese. I like to think of them as the
  British of the Far East.
KENTARO: You pay us too great a compliment.
SIR CLAUDE: Not at all. (*Turns to* MARY.) I understand you
  were a Mackenzie, is that correct?
MARY: Yes, sir.
SIR CLAUDE: Not related to the Achtarn Mackenzies by any
  chance?
MARY: No, my family's been settled in Edinburgh for
  generations.
SIR CLAUDE: Oh, well, can't be helped.
  (*At this point,* ISABELLE DE CHAMONPIERRE *joins them.*)
ISABELLE: I hope you two are ready to lead us in the first
  dance.
RICHARD: Certainly.

15

(ISABELLE *makes a sign to the all-Chinese orchestra and it strikes up with 'Tales from the Vienna Woods'.*
RICHARD *leads* MARY *out on to the floor. He turns out to be a superb dancer.* MARY *relaxes, her face intoxicated with pleasure. The room whirls around her.*)

INT. ENTRANCE HALL IN THE MANDARIN'S PALACE. DAY
MARY *has now changed out of her wedding dress and waits as* RICHARD *shakes hands with* SIR CLAUDE.
RICHARD: Thank you so much for taking the trouble, sir.
SIR CLAUDE: Not at all.
(*He turns to* MARY *and impulsively embraces her, kissing her on both cheeks.*)
MARY: Thank you.
SIR CLAUDE: God bless you, my dear young people, I wish you all the happiness in the world.

EXT. STREETS OF MUKDEN. EVENING
RICHARD *and* MARY *travel through the streets of Mukden in a droshky at dusk.*

EXT. DROSHKY. EVENING
RICHARD *draws* MARY *towards him.*
RICHARD: I'm sorry we're not having a proper honeymoon.
MARY: To be taken to a new house I've never seen. I think that's probably excitement enough.
RICHARD: Good.
MARY: Will I like it?
RICHARD: I don't know that it's particularly likeable.
(MARY *doesn't quite know what to make of this reply.*)

EXT. HOUSE OF THE DRAGON SCREEN. EVENING
The house, a large, low structure, is invisible behind thick walls.
RICHARD *and* MARY *are obliged to descend from the droshky some way from the red-painted front gate, which is approached down a narrow alley.*
RICHARD *tips the driver and escorts* MARY *down the alley, keeping her as far as possible away from the open drain which lies in the shadow of the wall. She can't fail to notice, however, the mound of*

rubbish rising from the drain not far from the gate, which is surmounted by a dead cat.
As they approach the large gate, a small hatch in it is opened by a handyman. He bows as RICHARD *and* MARY *step in through the hatch and closes it behind them.*

EXT. GARDEN. EVENING
RICHARD *addresses the handyman in Mandarin.*
RICHARD: Tell Yao Tsu we're here.
> (*The handyman bows again and scuttles off towards the house. The garden is dominated by the Dragon Screen, an eight-foot-high free-standing stone wall with a giant dragon carved on it, just visible, indeed menacingly so, in the dying light.*)
MARY: What on earth is that?
RICHARD: That's the Dragon Screen. It's supposed to keep out devils. Apparently, you see, Chinese devils are only capable of travelling in straight lines.
> (*They round the screen and approach the front door.*)

INT. HALLWAY. DRAGON SCREEN HOUSE. EVENING
YAO TSU *comes forward to greet them.*
MARY: Aren't you supposed to carry me across the threshold?
RICHARD: I don't want Yao Tsu to think I've gone completely off my head.
> (MARY's *face falls, but* RICHARD *doesn't seem to notice this. Instead, he stands back, waiting for her to enter the house first. As* MARY *enters the house, so* YAO TSU *falls to his knees, and to her surprise and, initially, alarm, he begins to grapple with one of her boots. Some new house-shoes are standing ready to replace the boots.*)
RICHARD: This is Yao Tsu, by the way, the houseboy.
MARY: Hello, Yao Tsu.
> (YAO TSU *looks up at her, his smile revealing a network of lines which show him to be older than he first seemed. Then he returns his attention to* MARY's *boot.*)
> I'm not sure this . . .
RICHARD: Let him do it.
> (*The boot is off and now* YAO TSU *guides* MARY's *foot into the house-shoe.*)

17

INT. MARY'S BEDROOM. EVENING
The gas is lit in the large, bleak bedroom. It contains a four-poster bed and a quantity of rudimentary furniture, including a baroque dressing-table.
RICHARD *shows* MARY *into the room.*
RICHARD: This is your bedroom.
MARY: Mine?
RICHARD: Mine is down the corridor.

INT. RICHARD'S BEDROOM. EVENING
RICHARD *shows* MARY *into a room which looks like something in a barracks: a camp bed, a canvas washbasin and a card table with shaving equipment and a small mirror above it. The window, which opens inwards, is ajar.*
RICHARD: Here's mine.
   (MARY *looks around with some alarm.*)
   I like things simple. And I can't sleep in a stuffy room.
MARY: I see.
RICHARD: There are nine other bedrooms. But they're hardly worth looking at, they're all empty, not even any beds.
   (MARY *wraps her arms round herself, against the cold.*)
   I asked Yao Tsu to tell Cook to prepare some soup.
MARY: I'm not very hungry.
RICHARD: Tired, I daresay.
MARY: Yes.
RICHARD: I'll give you ten minutes or so, that be enough?
   (*His voice is slightly strangled.*
   MARY *nods calmly and leaves the room.*)

INT. MARY'S BEDROOM. NIGHT
MARY *lies in bed, propped up by her pillow, in her nightdress, waiting. Presently, there's a knock at the door.*
MARY: Come in.
   (*Her voice is dry and hoarse. As she's clearing her throat,* RICHARD *enters. He's carrying a candlestick with a lighted candle. He turns the gas-lamp off. He puts the candle on the table on the far side of the bed from* MARY *and climbs into bed. Then he leans over and kisses her. She responds as best she may and then* RICHARD *sits up, slips out of his dressing gown, leans and blows out the candle. In the darkness the sounds of kissing;*

18

the rustle of MARY's *nightdress; then very soon after this, a low cry from* MARY. *Brief flashes of movement and grappling sounds; again, very soon, a discreet groan from* RICHARD; *and almost immediately, the movement and sound as he rolls off her. Then there's a moment's silence.*)

RICHARD: Goodnight, Mrs Collingsworth.

(*He leans over to kiss* MARY, *who responds numbly. Then he scrambles into his dressing gown, takes the candlestick and moves carefully, in the darkness, to the door, which, a moment later, he closes behind him.*

Close-up of MARY. *In the darkness, the movement is just visible, as she brings up a wrist to brush away a tear.*)

EXT. PLAINS. DAY
As seen from the train: the bleak Manchurian plains.

INT. DINING-ROOM. DAY
MARY *and* RICHARD *are eating breakfast in a silence broken, eventually, as* MARY *taps at her boiled egg.* RICHARD, *in uniform, sips at his tea.*

MARY: I'd have thought they might have given you a few days' leave.

RICHARD: I didn't ask for leave. I know what a busy time it is.

MARY: One day you must tell me about your work.

RICHARD: I don't think it would interest you very much.

MARY: I'm sure it would.

RICHARD: And of course a good deal of it is confidential.

(YAO TSU *appears with some more toast and takes away some of the used plates. He smiles deferentially at* MARY *as he leaves.*)

MARY: I'm not quite sure what I'm going to do with myself all day.

(RICHARD *nods sympathetically.*)

RICHARD: It's awkward, this place being so far out of the way. I'm afraid it's not really safe for you to go out at all.

MARY: Isn't it?

RICHARD: Not really.

(*He finishes his tea and leaves the table, turning back in the doorway as a thought strikes him.*)

Oh, there's one other thing. I've never been at my best in

the morning. Nothing to do with you, just a matter of temperament. So I thought it might be better if in the future Yao Tsu brings you breakfast on a tray. In your room.

MARY: Just as you like.

(RICHARD *nods an acknowledgement and leaves the room.*)

INT. DRAWING-ROOM. DAY
A large, gloomy room, mostly furnished in dark wood and red plush and dominated by an enormous coal stove.
YAO TSU *has been serving tea to* MARY *and* ISABELLE DE CHAMONPIERRE. *As he leaves the room,* MARY *picks up a plate of rock cakes and offers it to* ISABELLE.

MARY: Have one of these: I don't think they're very good.

(ISABELLE *declines, shaking her head.*)

ISABELLE: How is he, your cook?

MARY: All right, I suppose. I've never met him.

ISABELLE: What?

MARY: Richard says I should keep away from the kitchen.

(ISABELLE *shakes her head, incredulous. She gets up and moves around the room for a while, peering critically at whatever monstrosities catch her eye, before coming to rest by the gigantic stove.*)

ISABELLE: This monster stove, I suppose you could make it look quite amusing when you redecorate.

MARY: I don't know if we can afford to redecorate.

(ISABELLE *looks sharply at* MARY *for a moment.*)

ISABELLE: When I married Armand it was agreed he would furnish our house out of the dowry.

MARY: We don't have dowries in Britain any more: the custom's died out.

ISABELLE: I thought your family owned a factory . . .

(*She breaks off, aware from* MARY's *expression that she has overstepped the mark.* MARY *says nothing: she looks completely winded.*)

I'm sorry. I always wonder how the British won such a great Empire, when all the really important subjects in life – food, money, everything like that – they are incapable even to mention.

20

INT. BEDROOM. NIGHT
Darkness. Once again, RICHARD *rolls off* MARY, *climbs into his dressing gown, picks up his candlestick and makes his way to the door. He's almost there before* MARY *speaks.*
MARY: Goodnight.
RICHARD: Yes.
   (*He leaves the room.*)

EXT. APPROACHES TO TEMPLE COMPLEX. DAY
It's a lovely day in early summer. RICHARD *and* MARY, *in separate rickshaws, are drawn up the hill towards a group of three or four temples, one brightly painted, the others in varying states of disrepair.*

EXT. MAIN TEMPLE. DAY
RICHARD *dismounts and helps* MARY *down from her rickshaw.*
RICHARD: This is the only temple in use. They rent out the
   others for summer villas. Funny old religion.

INT. TEMPLE. DAY
The gloom of the interior is brightened by the brilliantly painted walls and ceiling-beams. A priest conducts RICHARD *and* MARY *through an outer room. As the priest pauses in the doorway of the inner sanctum to bow to the altar,* MARY *is horrified to see* RICHARD *take a lapis lazuli dish from a side table and slip it into his inside pocket. She's about to protest, but* RICHARD *puts a finger to his lips and follows the priest into the next room.*

INT. BEDROOM. DRAGON SCREEN HOUSE. NIGHT
RICHARD *is putting on his dressing gown in the dark.*
MARY: Can't you stay for a while?
RICHARD: Yes, all right.
MARY: Light the candle.
   (*There are some matches in his dressing-gown pocket. Presently he strikes one, and lights his candle. Then he allows* MARY *to snuggle into the crook of his arm.*
   Silence.
   Eventually RICHARD *makes a strange gesture with his free arm, intended to indicate the bed and the bedroom.*)

21

RICHARD: All this . . . bedroom stuff, it doesn't matter in the least.
MARY: No. Of course it doesn't.
(*But it evidently does. To both of them.*)

INT. DINING-ROOM. EVENING
MARY *is eating dinner alone: presently,* RICHARD *arrives, attended by a slightly flustered* YAO TSU.
MARY *looks up from her soup.*
MARY: I didn't wait this time.
RICHARD: So I see.
MARY: Have you been playing cards at the Club?
(RICHARD *doesn't answer for the moment. Instead, he turns to dismiss* YAO TSU.)
RICHARD: Whisky, Yao.
(YAO TSU *leaves the room and* RICHARD *sits at the table.*)
Not this evening, no.
(*He pauses importantly.*
MARY *is watching* RICHARD, *her expression cool.*
He turns to her.)
Our intelligence is that war will break out between Russia and Japan within a few weeks. I've been ordered to report to Port Arthur in the New Year, which is one of the best possible places to be. I'm bound to be right in the thick of things.
MARY: How wonderful for you.
(RICHARD *hurries on excitedly, oblivious to the edge in her voice.*)
RICHARD: I know, theoretically, we support the Japanese, but it obviously makes much better sense from the point of view of experience to be an Observer on the winning side.
MARY: You're convinced the Russians will win.
RICHARD: Of course they will, they have more than a million men in their standing army. It'll all be over in two or three months at the outside.
(YAO TSU *arrives with* RICHARD's *whisky and soda, which he begins to gulp down.*)
MARY: You love the idea of going away, don't you?
(RICHARD *looks up, slightly surprised by her tone.*)
RICHARD: I consider this an important opportunity. Where else in the world could I get first-hand day-to-day experience of

a war? It is my profession, and I take it seriously. That doesn't mean I won't miss you. Of course I will.
(*He pauses and looks up at* MARY, *but* MARY *says nothing.*)
I've arranged for the Bank to take care of the bills while I'm away.

MARY: I was wondering . . . I meant to talk to you, I've been meaning to . . .

RICHARD: What about?

MARY: About an allowance. About giving me an allowance.
(*Silence.* RICHARD *looks at her for a moment.*)

RICHARD: I understood your mother had made some provision.

MARY: She gave me fifty pounds. It can't last for ever.

RICHARD: No, quite.
(*He finishes his whisky.*)
I can't bear talking about money. Let me think about it while I'm away.

MARY: Three months on my own here . . .

RICHARD: I'll write as often as I can manage.

INT. DINING-ROOM IN THE MANDARIN'S PALACE. NIGHT.
1904
Another dinner party at the Mandarin's Palace. Once again, there are six or eight guests, but this time RICHARD *is not among them.* MARY *sits towards the centre of the table talking to her neighbour, who turns out to be* KENTARO KURIHAMA. ISABELLE *is at the head of the table, conversing animatedly in French.*

MARY: Do *you* believe there's going to be a war, Count?

KENTARO: I hope not; war has always seemed to me to be an exceedingly blunt instrument.

MARY: You speak such wonderful English. Where did you learn?

KENTARO: My father sent me to study at Oxford.

MARY: Did you enjoy it?

KENTARO: It was most fascinating.

MARY: That sounds to me like a diplomatic answer.
(KENTARO *looks at her for a moment as if assessing whether he should elaborate.*)

KENTARO: I did not find them very serious. It was difficult to understand why some of your upper-class young men enjoyed behaving so badly. We are taught that the more

23

important your position in society, the more self-discipline you must exercise. A cultural difference, I suppose.

MARY: I imagine so.

KENTARO: I saw more evidence of it after the Siege of Peking. The looting.

MARY: The English were looting?

KENTARO: Yes, all the European armies. Only in the Japanese army was it forbidden. Anyone found doing so was shot.

MARY: I see.

KENTARO: Please do not think I intend to insult the English.

MARY: I'm a Scot. We quite often feel much the same way.

(*She smiles at him and, after a moment's surprise, he responds.*)

KENTARO: Your Ambassador called us the British of the Far East.

MARY: I remember.

KENTARO: I think he thought this was a compliment.

MARY: I think he did.

KENTARO: I do not deny it, we have our own codes – but very different from yours, I believe.

MARY: I'm afraid I know very little about your country.

KENTARO: You must read – if you are interested, I mean – you must read Lafcadio Hearn.

MARY: Who?

KENTARO: Lafcadio Hearn. He has been living in Japan about ten years and writing all about us. He sees only our good side, so naturally I am a great admirer of his.

(*He's made her smile once again.*)

INT. DRAWING-ROOM IN THE MANDARIN'S PALACE. NIGHT
MARY *comes to with a start to find* KENTARO *looking down at her.*

KENTARO: Your husband is away?

MARY: Yes. In Port Arthur.

(KENTARO *considers her for a moment before speaking.*)

KENTARO: I wish it had been possible for me to spend some time with him but I had the impression he was not a great admirer of our Anglo-Japanese Alliance.

MARY: You don't seem too convinced about it either.

(*He is surprised into another smile.*)

KENTARO: I will have to leave Mukden soon.

MARY: Why?

KENTARO: When the war begins, it would not do for me to be here, behind enemy lines.

INT. DRAWING-ROOM IN DRAGON SCREEN HOUSE. DAY
MARY *sits working at some embroidery. Presently,* YAO TSU *comes into the room with a parcel which he hands to her. As he leaves the room,* MARY *tears off the brown paper and discovers a book. She looks at it. It's* Kokoro *by Lafcadio Hearn, in the rather beautiful 1896 American edition. She opens the cover, but there's nothing written on the fly-leaf. Nor is there any card. To all intents and purposes, it's an entirely anonymous gift.*

EXT. GARDEN. DRAGON SCREEN HOUSE. DAY
It's high summer. MARY, *protected by a wide-brimmed hat, is picking flowers, which she lays in a basket.*
She looks up, surprised, as ISABELLE DE CHAMONPIERRE *appears round the Dragon Screen. She straightens up and they embrace, kissing each other on both cheeks. She's pleased to see* ISABELLE, *who, however, seems under something of a strain.*
MARY: This is a pleasant surprise.
ISABELLE: Armand arrived back today.
MARY: Well, that's good. Isn't it?
ISABELLE: He says the Japanese have entirely surrounded Port Arthur. It's under siege.
MARY: Oh.
ISABELLE: Of course, I'm sure Richard will be safe. It's just that he won't be able to get out of the city. He may be there for months.
MARY: I see.
ISABELLE: I came to ask you to come and stay with us for a while.
(MARY *hesitates, but only for a short time.*)
MARY: Well, perhaps, just for a few days . . .

EXT. HILLS NEAR MUKDEN. DAY
A picnic has been set out on a rug in the shade of a bamboo plantation not far from the foot of a waterfall. MARY *and* ISABELLE DE CHAMONPIERRE *sit on another rug, their parasols to hand.* MARY *looks up as* ARMAND *approaches. He has a beautiful leaf in his hand.*

25

ARMAND: Look, I have found a gingko tree.

MARY: What is that?

ARMAND: A very interesting tree.

ISABELLE: Interesting to you.

ARMAND: It's not usually found so far North, although before the Ice Age it was common in Northern Europe. They have found fossils of the leaf in the Isle of Mull.

(*He hands the leaf to* MARY. MARY *looks at it, filled with a sudden melancholy, as* ARMAND *goes to the pool at the foot of the waterfall, reaches down and produces a bottle of champagne. He tests its temperature.*)

Pas mal.

(*He opens the champagne as he moves back towards* MARY. ISABELLE *hands him a glass.*)

It is also known as the maidenhair tree, for, I suppose, an obvious reason.

(MARY *looks away, colouring.*)

It's such a beautiful day, we should drink a toast.

(*He distributes the champagne.*)

An end to war.

MARY: I don't think Richard would drink to that.

ARMAND: Perhaps not, but we can if we want to.

(*They raise their glasses.*)

EXT. HILLS NEAR MUKDEN. DAY

The picnic is over. ARMAND *lies with his head in* ISABELLE'S *lap.* MARY *is watching them, her expression somewhat perturbed.* ARMAND, *half-asleep, reaches up to caress* ISABELLE, *who lays aside her embroidery to cradle his head.*

MARY *rises to her feet and* ISABELLE *looks up at her.*

MARY: I think I'll go for a walk.

(*She picks up her parasol and hurries away.*)

EXT. APPROACHES TO THE TEMPLE COMPLEX. DAY

MARY *moves up the hill towards the temple complex. Approaching her is a gang of coolies under the supervision of a mounted Cossack officer.* MARY *hardly glances at him, but as they pass, the Cossack catches her eye and salutes smartly.*

COSSACK: Bonjour, mademoiselle.

MARY: Bonjour.

(She has hardly spoken, when her eyes register absolute amazement. One of the work-party, despite his pigtail and drab blue fatigues, is unmistakably KENTARO KURIHAMA. *He realizes immediately that she has recognized him and transmits with an infinitesimal shake of the head, that she should not acknowledge him.* MARY *understands the message and hurries on, more astonished than ever.)*

INT. MARY'S ROOM IN THE MANDARIN'S PALACE. DAY
MARY *sits, turning over in her hands the lapis lazuli dish. She looks up as, from a neighbouring room, come the unmistakable sounds of lovemaking. After a moment's hesitation, she reaches for her parasol and leaves the room.*

EXT. THE MANDARIN'S PALACE. DAY
MARY *hurries across the garden and through the elaborate 'Lion' gate.*

EXT. MAIN TEMPLE. DAY
MARY *lowers her parasol and enters the cool dark of the temple.*

INT. TEMPLE. DAY
There's a man in a black kimono praying in the outer room. He seems absorbed and, after glancing at him, MARY *feels confident enough to do what she has come to do: to replace the lapis lazuli dish stolen by* RICHARD. *This done, she hurries out of the room. The man in the kimono looks up as she leaves: it's* KENTARO.

EXT. TEMPLE. DAY
MARY *puts up her parasol. As she does so, she's considerably startled by* KENTARO's *voice.*
KENTARO: Thank you, Mrs Collingsworth.
   (Before she can answer, he's beside her.)
   I believe you saved my life yesterday.
MARY: What are you doing here?
KENTARO: One of the reasons the war is going so well for us is the European's well-known inability to tell us apart. It means we are a great deal better informed than the Russians could ever be.
MARY: So you mean you're . . .

27

KENTARO: Here as a spy. That's right. Assessing the strength
and dispositions of the enemy.
MARY: I see.
(*Silence.*)
KENTARO: I know it's not necessary to ask you to tell no one
you have seen me.
MARY: Of course not.
KENTARO: I am living in one of the disused temples. There's a
Chinese who looks after me and gets me everything I need.
MARY: Is he reliable?
KENTARO: He hates the Russians. They killed his father.
MARY: I see.
KENTARO: But also, I pay him enough to make him very
reliable.
(*Silence.* KENTARO *looks at* MARY *for a moment. She's
uncomfortably aware of his fixed gaze.*)
MARY: I'm staying with the Chamonpierres.
KENTARO: Come at four tomorrow: I will give you some tea.
MARY: I . . .
(*She turns away, blushing, then murmurs, almost inaudibly.*)
I don't think . . .
(*She turns and hurries away down the hill, speaking with her
back to him.*)
I'll see.

INT. MARY'S ROOM IN THE MANDARIN'S PALACE. NIGHT
The room is flooded with moonlight. MARY, *sleepless, shifts and
turns.*

INT. UNITED FREE CHURCH OF SCOTLAND. DAY
The wedding: KENTARO, *in the congregation, stares impassively at*
MARY.

EXT. TEMPLE PRECINCTS. DAY
MARY *approaches the main temple, moving like a sleepwalker.
Suddenly, a Chinese appears from the shadow of the walls and
indicates that she should follow him.*

EXT. DISUSED TEMPLE. DAY
The Chinese disappears around a corner. MARY *follows him, but*

he's vanished. Instead, KENTARO *stands in the low doorway to the temple.*

KENTARO: Please. Come in.

INT. DISUSED TEMPLE. DAY

The temple, decaying and neglected, but somehow made welcomingly domestic by KENTARO's *simple arrangements. There's a futon on the floor, and various cushions and low tables. A vase containing a few simply arranged dried grasses stands in a recess: above it, a painting which consists of a vertical line of ideograms. Everything has been prepared for tea, including small dishes on the tables containing gelatinous pink squares of perfumed candy.* MARY *stands for a moment, taking in the scene.*

KENTARO: Sit.

> (*He indicates one of the cushions.* MARY *sits down obediently, her back straight.* KENTARO *transfers the water to the teapot by means of an elegant wooden ladle.*)

MARY: Can I help you with something?

KENTARO: No, no.

> (*She watches as he mixes the tea with a brush of birch twigs and pours it into a pair of small earthenware bowls. This done, he brings the bowls over to her and ceremoniously places one on the floor in front of her. He settles himself on the other cushion, placing his own bowl carefully on the floor in front of him. Then he looks up at her.*)

Now. Shall we take some tea first?

EXT. MANDARIN'S PALACE. DAWN

It's hardly light.

INT. MARY'S ROOM IN THE MANDARIN'S PALACE. DAWN

MARY *wakes and jumps out of bed, starts to get dressed.*

EXT. APPROACHES TO THE TEMPLE COMPLEX. DAWN

MARY, *alone, hurries up the hill.*

EXT. DISUSED TEMPLE. DAWN

MARY *rounds the corner to see* KENTARO, *his eyes closed, in a*

spotless white kimono, sitting in the lotus position on a small straw
mat. He is praying, his prayers interspersed with low bows.
MARY *watches, fascinated.*
He comes to an end, opens his eyes and sees her.
MARY: I'm sorry. I didn't mean to disturb you.
KENTARO: No, no.
MARY: Have you . . . finished?
KENTARO: I was praying for forgiveness from the souls of those
    of my men who were killed in battle.
MARY: I'm sure it couldn't have been your fault.
KENTARO: Perhaps I should have given better orders.
    (KENTARO *rises to his feet and* MARY *hurries over to him.*
    MARY *and* KENTARO *embrace.*)
    I have many things still to do. Can you come back again
    this afternoon?
MARY: Oh, yes.
KENTARO: I hope so, because tonight I must return through the
    lines.
    (*Silence. He looks down at her.*)
    Come in for a few minutes.
    (*He leads her slowly into the house.*)

INT. DINING-ROOM IN THE MANDARIN'S PALACE. DAY
ARMAND: I thought we might take a little expedition to the east
    this afternoon. There's a species of magnolia I haven't
    found yet, and I understand there's also a spectacular view
    of the city.
MARY: I think, if you don't mind . . . I rather feel the need to
    be on my own this afternoon.
ARMAND: Of course.
    (*But* ISABELLE *is looking at* MARY, *her expression puzzled.*)

INT. DISUSED TEMPLE. DAY
MARY *and* KENTARO *lie on the futon, entwined in each other's*
arms.
MARY: I used to look at other couples and wonder if there
    wasn't some kind of secret happiness they shared. Now I
    understand.
    (*She turns to brush his cheek with her lips.*)
KENTARO: I don't want to go back to the war.

30

(*She covers his mouth with her fingers.*)
I am ashamed.
(*He reaches up and brushes the hair out of her eyes.*)
But not as ashamed as I should be.
MARY: And you're not sorry?
KENTARO: Of course not.
MARY: I'll never be sorry.
(*Tears start to run down* MARY's *face.*)
KENTARO: You must not cry, Mary.
(*She shakes her head, the tears still flowing.*)
Come here.
(*He draws her to him.*)

EXT. TEMPLE PRECINTS. EVENING
The sun has set. MARY *hurries down the road, half running,
sobbing.*

INT. DRAWING-ROOM IN THE MANDARIN'S PALACE.
EVENING
MARY *bursts into the room. The* CHAMONPIERRES *look up, silent,
glasses in their hands.* ISABELLE *is smoking. She looks angry.*
MARY *does her best to compose herself.*
MARY: I'm sorry. I got lost.
ISABELLE: Yes. This is what Armand and I have decided.
     (*Her expression is cool.* MARY *tries to smile at* ARMAND, *but
     he looks away.*)

EXT. HOUSE OF THE DRAGON SCREEN. DAY. 1905
*The house and garden are locked in by a layer of deep snow and ice.
Still, grey day.*

INT. DRAWING-ROOM. DAY
MARY *sits huddled by the stove.*
She looks up to hear a quarrel erupting in the hall between YAO TSU
and ISABELLE DE CHAMONPIERRE. ISABELLE, *not to be
deflected, arrives in the doorway.* MARY *rises to her feet: so that we
realize, at the same moment as* ISABELLE, *that she is five months
pregnant.* ISABELLE's *hand goes to her mouth.*
ISABELLE: *Oh, mon Dieu!*
MARY: Yes, I'm sorry, I told Yao Tsu not to let anyone in.

31

ISABELLE: *Ma petite.*
> (*She hurries across the room and takes* MARY *in her arms.*
> *Eventually* ISABELLE *releases* MARY *and looks down at her.*)
> Why didn't you tell me? If you told me sooner, we could
> have done something.

MARY: No.

ISABELLE: You English. Don't you even learn how to take
> precautions?

MARY: I didn't want to be cautious.

ISABELLE: Whose is it? Do you want to tell me?
> (MARY *looks at her, considering whether or not to confide in*
> *her. Eventually, tears springing to her eyes, she shakes her*
> *head.*)

EXT. GARDEN. DAY
The snow is receding somewhat. The handyman attacks it with a
shovel.

INT. DRAWING-ROOM. DAY
MARY *stands at the window, behind the net curtain, looking out.*
She is wearing a loose-fitting house-coat. Her expression changes and
her hand moves from her stomach to cover her mouth.

EXT. GARDEN. DAY
RICHARD *strides towards the house, taking no notice of the bowing*
handyman.

INT. FRONT HALL/DRAWING-ROOM. DAY
As RICHARD *enters the house,* MARY *appears in the doorway of the*
drawing-room. He begins hurrying towards her, then stops dead,
suddenly aware of her condition.

MARY: Richard.

RICHARD: Whose is it?
> (MARY *does not answer for a moment.*)

MARY: I can't . . .

RICHARD: Or don't you know?
> (*He turns and runs abruptly down the corridor leading to his*
> *room.*)

INT. CORRIDOR OUTSIDE MARY'S BEDROOM. DAY
MARY *hurries after* RICHARD *as he vanishes into his room. She waits a moment, uncertain. Then she hears from his room the sound of vomiting.*

INT. MARY'S BEDROOM. DAY
MARY *sits at her dressing table.* RICHARD *bursts into the room.*
RICHARD: I want you out of here by tonight.
MARY: Where should I go?
RICHARD: I'll put you in the hotel until I can arrange you a
　　　passage back to London. I've a good mind to send you
　　　steerage.
MARY: Do, if you want to.
　　　(RICHARD *paces up and down in silence for a moment.*)
RICHARD: You needn't think your mother's going to get out of
　　　our arrangement.
MARY: What?
RICHARD: She agreed to pay me three hundred pounds a year as
　　　long as we're married.
　　　(MARY *looks up, thunderstruck.*)

INT. MACKENZIE HOUSE IN EDINBURGH. EVENING
As before. No sound. MARY'*s point of view, as her mother leans to whisper in* RICHARD'*s ear.*

INT. MARY'S BEDROOM. DAY
RICHARD'*s face, contorted with rage.*
RICHARD: And I've no intention of giving you a divorce.
MARY: But that's almost half of her income.
RICHARD: It's what she agreed.
MARY: I had no idea.
RICHARD: I have it in writing.
MARY: Then it's between you and her.
　　　(*Silence, as* MARY *comes to terms with his revelation; it is
　　　interrupted by a cry from* RICHARD.)
RICHARD: Whose is it? Tell me!
MARY: I can't tell you.
RICHARD: Why did you do it?
　　　(*There is no answer from* MARY, *she simply looks around the
　　　room.* RICHARD *knows what the answer is: he colours and*

*looks down. Then he leaves the room as abruptly as he has
entered it.)*

EXT. HOUSE OF THE DRAGON SCREEN. EVENING
MARY *is drawn away in the first of three rickshaws. Her luggage is
in the second. The handyman is in the third. She looks up and sees*
RICHARD, *staring down from a lighted upstairs window.*

INT. MUKDEN STATION. DAY
*The station is guarded by Japanese soldiers, and the activity on the
platform makes it quite clear that the Japanese have taken over the
city.*
A Chinese porter is stowing MARY's *bags into the guard's van under
her supervision, when she becomes aware of a young Japanese
soldier standing at her elbow. He is* YOSHIO NOMURA. *He bows to
her.*
NOMURA: Nomura Yoshio. I am here orders from Colonel
    Kurihama.
MARY: Is he here?
NOMURA: No. But I have orders. You must go to Dairen.
MARY: I know. I have to ship out from there. Back to London.
NOMURA: No.
MARY: No?
NOMURA: From Dairen you will go to Shimonoseki.
MARY: Where?
NOMURA: In Japan.
MARY: What?
NOMURA: Yes. You must live in Tokyo.
    (Silence, as MARY *thinks for a moment, frowning in
    concentration. When she looks back at* NOMURA, *he hands her
    some documents.)*
    Here is your tickets.

34

TWO

INT. CUSTOMS SHED AT SHIMONOSEKI. NIGHT
MARY's trunk and suitcases are being chalked by a customs official.
She looks around, more than a little apprehensive.
A Japanese family is next in line, the mother carrying a CHILD *of*
about four, who's staring at MARY.
MARY smiles tentatively at the CHILD. *By way of response, he*
points at her and speaks, very clearly, one word:
CHILD: *Ijin.*
> (*The mother hushes the* CHILD *and moves off, as* MARY *is*
> *startled by the arrival of a young* JAPANESE SOLDIER.)
SOLDIER: Mrs Collingsworth?
> (MARY *shakes her head.*)
MARY: No.
> (*The soldier frowns, bewildered.*)
> Miss Mackenzie.

EXT. SHIMONOSEKI STREETS. NIGHT
MARY, in a rickshaw, follows the young SOLDIER. *Next, in*
another rickshaw, her luggage.

INT. FIRST-CLASS COMPARTMENT. NIGHT
MARY is shown into her compartment. She pauses in the doorway,
surprised to see, in the far corner, a Japanese woman in Western
clothes, white blouse, dark skirt, with, however carelessly displayed,
an air of distinction. Her expression is lively and inquisitive and,
though her age is difficult to judge, she seems not much older than
MARY. This is BARONESS AIKO ONNODERA. *The soldier speaks to*
her in Japanese.
SOLDIER: This is the woman, Baroness.
AIKO: Thank you, you may go.
> (*The* SOLDIER *bows and leaves.*
> MARY *stands, just inside the door, slightly at a loss.* AIKO
> *assesses her shrewdly for a moment before speaking, this time in*
> *English, which she speaks quite fluently.*)
> Do sit down and make yourself comfortable.
> (MARY *sits opposite her, still uncertain.*)

35

I know who you are, but perhaps you've not been told
anything about me?

MARY: No, I'm afraid I haven't.

AIKO: My name is Aiko Onnodera, Baroness, not that it matters
– Kurihama and I hardly agree on anything, but we have
known each other since childhood and saw a good deal of
each other in England.

MARY: Oh, I see, he's asked you to meet me.

AIKO: And fortunately I was able to, thanks to my early release
from prison.

(MARY *blinks at her, seems about to speak, then thinks better
of it.*)

EXT. RAILWAY TRACK. NIGHT
The train passes through mountainous landscape.

INT. RESTAURANT CAR. NIGHT
MARY *and* AIKO *are eating,* MARY *with some difficulty, hesitating
dubiously before tackling each unrecognizable component of the
meal.*

AIKO: You are too polite to ask why I was in prison, but I
expect you would like to know. I was protesting outside a
newspaper office in Tokyo, and I saw this journalist who
wrote in his column that Japanese women would not have
the vote in a thousand years time. It seems I hit him with
my banner.

(MARY *is bemused, but can't help smiling.*)
The women I met in England were very determined and
I'm sure there will be a great deal of trouble in the next few
years, but none of them seemed to realize how fortunate
she was compared to us Japanese.

MARY: I've never really thought about these things.

AIKO: My dear, you are now in a country where there isn't even
universal suffrage for men. The first time I was arrested
was for trying to get in to listen to a debate in the Diet. In
court I asked if they were afraid of us finding out how
boring their debates were. They doubled the fine.

MARY: You're what my mother used to call a professional
agitator.

AIKO: Tradition is even more important in my country than it is

36

in yours, and my family has a tradition of dissent. My grandfather made a passionate speech in the Diet denouncing the power of the Army and the amount of money it wasted. The following night he was assassinated. They broke into the house and cut him to pieces.
(*Silence.* MARY *considers her companion, now eating with skill and speed.*)

MARY: Are you married?

AIKO: No, I'm like you. I'm an outcast.
(MARY *is a little shocked by* AIKO's *bluntness.* AIKO *continues, however, unaware of this.*)
To be a divorced woman is much more of a disgrace here than it ever could be in Europe.

MARY: I'm not divorced.

AIKO: Yes, but I am. Onnodera was very embarrassed by my politics, but he is a tolerant man; in the end there was something else which affected him far more deeply.

MARY: What was that?

AIKO: I am barren. I can never have a child.
(*She looks away; now it's she who, for the first time, is showing signs of constraint; and* MARY, *only too aware of her own condition, can find nothing to say.*)

INT. COMPARTMENT. DAWN
MARY *wakes, as light begins to steal into the compartment. Opposite her,* AIKO *is still asleep.* MARY *moves towards the window, raises a corner of the blind and peeps out.*

EXT. RAILWAY. DAWN
The train passes, as dawn breaks over the Inland Sea. The blind is raised and we see MARY *looking out.*

INT. COMPARTMENT. DAWN
MARY *looks out of the window, thoughtful, dazzled by the beautiful landscapes of the Inland Sea, trying to adjust to the spectacle of her first day in Japan.*

INT. COMPARTMENT. DAY
MARY *looks up sharply as* AIKO *lets herself back into the compartment.*

MARY: Kentaro, do you know what his intentions are?
AIKO: You haven't heard from him?
MARY: Nothing, no, I just felt . . . whatever it was would be
    better than crawling back to Scotland.
AIKO: Well, he has . . . I am to take you to a house he has
    found for you in Tsukiji in Tokyo, which is one of the
    areas where foreigners usually live. You will have two
    servants and . . .
MARY: Yes, but does he mean, well, to marry me? Or . . .
    (*Silence.* AIKO *looks at her for a moment.*)
AIKO: You don't know.
MARY: What?
AIKO: He is married. He has four children.

EXT. MARY'S HOUSE IN TSUKIJI. DAY
A pretty one-storey house with a small garden containing an
ornamental pond.
Enough time for the image to register.

EXT. FRONT ENTRANCE TO THE HOUSE. DAY
As MARY *and* AIKO *arrive in separate rickshaws, two women*
emerge from the house: the maid, MISAO, *a pretty, smiling girl of*
about nineteen, and the cook, FUKUDA, *an older and much dourer*
figure. They bow deeply as AIKO *leads* MARY *down the short front*
path.
AIKO: This is Misao San, your maid, and Fukuda, the cook.
    (MARY *tries to shake hands, but her hand is not taken. Instead*
    the bows proliferate.)
MARY: The first thing I must do is learn the language.
AIKO: Perhaps.
MARY: If I had a dictionary, I could communicate with them.
    They can read?
    (AIKO *frowns, a flicker of annoyance in her eyes.*)
AIKO: Of course they can read. This is not one of those
    backward countries, you know.
MARY: I'm sorry.
    (AIKO *softens, and puts out a hand, which* MARY *takes.*)
AIKO: I'll send a rickshaw for you tomorrow and take you to
    meet your doctor.
MARY: You've been very kind, thank you.

(AIKO *hesitates at the gate and looks back at* MARY.)

AIKO: I should tell you, women of your class are not supposed
    to go out on their own.

MARY: What class is that?

AIKO: You will find there are many restrictions in the life
    of a . . .

MARY: A what?

AIKO: A concubine.

MARY: Is that what I am?

AIKO: The term is purely technical.

MARY: Oh, well, that's all right, then.

    (AIKO *hesitates, then bows and climbs into the rickshaw.*)

INT. LIVING-ROOM IN MARY'S HOUSE. NIGHT
*The plain, eight-mat room is heated by a low brazier and lit by
electricity.* MARY's *ready for bed and her quilts have been laid out
on the floor. She rests a hand on her stomach, her expression
frightened and vulnerable. She switches off the light and climbs
laboriously in between the quilts. From outside the house comes a
strange clattering sound, accompanied by a melancholy, high-pitched
call.* MARY, *lit by the glow of the brazier, listens wide-eyed with
apprehension.*

EXT. MARY'S HOUSE. NIGHT
*The house is entirely encased in wooden shutters. Outside, the night-
watchman passes. He strikes a pair of wooden clappers together and
calls out that all is well.*

EXT. FRONT ENTRANCE. DAY
MISAO *hurries out of the house in pursuit of* MARY, *who turns and
shakes her head at her.*

MARY: No. You stay.

    (MISAO *smiles and inclines her head but keeps on advancing.*)
    No, I'm just going for a walk. You stay here.
    (MISAO *hesitates and watches as* MARY *leaves the garden,
    closing the gate behind her. Then she sets off in pursuit.*)

EXT. BANK OF THE SUMIDA RIVER. DAY
MARY *walks along the bank, looking at the river below.* MISAO
follows, at a discreet distance. Passers-by stare curiously at MARY,

39

not acknowledging her. She stops to look at the wares spread out on
one of the stalls set up on the riverbank.
The various goods for sale – tea-towels, fans, bath towels,
lithographs, etc. – are all painted with garish scenes from the
Russian–Japanese War. A tray of hatpins catches MARY's
attention. She fetches one out, the top of which is a Japanese and
British flag intercrossed.
Then she becomes aware of the number of people watching her –
and, once again, of the muttered word, 'ijin'.

INT. AIKO'S ROOM IN THE OKATSU HOTEL. DAY
A rather seedy hotel room stocked with Western furniture of a heavy
old-fashioned type. It also contains a printing press and a mass of
different-coloured leaflets.
AIKO *crosses to hand* MARY *a book.*
AIKO: Your dictionary.
MARY: Thank you.
　　(She leafs through it as AIKO *pours tea, not looking at* MARY.)
AIKO: I have to go away tomorrow.
MARY: Oh?
AIKO: On a speaking tour. I try to talk to women in all the
　　villages.
MARY: What about?
AIKO: Their condition. Japanese women are expected to observe
　　the three obediences, do you know about this?
MARY: No.
AIKO: First they must be obedient to their parents, then to their
　　husband and his parents, and finally when they are old,
　　they must obey their sons.
MARY: I see.
AIKO: Obedience is a habit it is not easy to break. And most of
　　them are told by their husbands or fathers or sons not to
　　come to my meetings.
MARY: It sounds like an uphill struggle.
　　*(*AIKO *hands her a bowl of tea.)*
AIKO: The further you get from Tokyo, the more oppression
　　you find; and the more oppressed they are, the less they
　　understand what you are telling them. But I feel the least I
　　can do is try.
　　(She sips her tea.)

MARY: What does '*ijin*' mean?
AIKO: *Ijin?*
MARY: I've heard it a lot. Does it mean 'hello'?
AIKO: No. No, it doesn't.
MARY: Well, what does it mean?
  (AIKO *looks at* MARY, *pity in her eyes.*)
AIKO: It means 'foreigner'.
  (MARY *looks away, upset.*)

INT. DOCTOR IKEDA'S SURGERY. DAY
A youngish Japanese doctor, DOCTOR IKEDA, *has just finished examining* MARY. *He removes his gloves as she answers his questions.*
IKEDA: I expect you're tired?
MARY: Yes, exhausted most of the time, and quite a lot of vomiting.
IKEDA: Any bleeding?
MARY: Some, yes, just a few spots.
  (IKEDA *crosses to his desk, begins making notes.*)
IKEDA: I think you should take plenty of rest. And stay home.
  (MARY *frowns, slightly alarmed by a hint of menace in his voice.*)

EXT. FRONT ENTRANCE TO MARY'S HOUSE. DAY
The rickshaw drivers wait outside the gate, by which AIKO *has paused.*
AIKO: I won't come in.
  (MARY *turns, once again somewhat frightened.*)
MARY: I wish you weren't going away.
AIKO: I also.
  (MARY *embraces her impulsively:* AIKO *is startled, but touched.*)
MARY: Thank you for everything.
  (AIKO *turns away abruptly and climbs into the rickshaw.*)

EXT. VERANDA OF MARY'S HOUSE. DAY
It's early summer and MARY, *now significantly more pregnant, sits on a wicker chair on a corner of the veranda, reading the* Japan Advertiser, *an English-language newspaper, the headline of which*

proclaims a great Japanese victory in the Battle of Tsushima and the destruction of the Russian Baltic fleet.
She looks up as there's a sharp rap on the front door. By moving a few feet and peering round the angle of the house, she's able to see the front door.

EXT. FRONT OF MARY'S HOUSE. DAY
MISS ALICIA BASSETT-HILL, a grey-haired lady, whose severe skirt and sensible shoes would not look out of place in an Oxfordshire parish hall, waits outside the door. When MISAO opens it, ALICIA booms out in Japanese, using that particular loud and patient tone adopted by English people speaking a foreign language.
ALICIA: Good morning. Is your mistress at home?
MISAO: Would you mind waiting a moment?

EXT. VERANDA. MARY'S HOUSE. DAY
As MISAO arrives on the veranda, MARY is there to intercept her. She puts her finger to her lips and shakes her head violently. MISAO bows minimally in acknowledgement and vanishes.

EXT. FRONT OF MARY'S HOUSE. DAY
MISAO reappears.
Dialogue in Japanese.
MISAO: I'm afraid nobody is in.
ALICIA: Well, would you give her my card? And these too, if you would be so kind.
(She hands over her card and a tin of Huntley and Palmer's assorted biscuits.)
MISAO: Certainly, madam.
ALICIA: Good day.

EXT. VERANDA. MARY'S HOUSE. DAY
MARY hears the sound of ALICIA's confident footsteps as they die away. MISAO appears and hands MARY the tin of biscuits and a card which reads: 'MISS ALICIA BASSETT-HILL, Society for the Propagation of the Christian Gospel', and an address. MARY studies the card, turning it over to look at the Japanese characters on the back, frowning as MISAO giggles in the background.

INT. BOX IN THE KABUKI. DAY
The card, in AIKO's *hand. She hands it back to* MARY *as she speaks, and gradually it becomes clear that the two of them are in a small box at the back of the Kabuki Theatre.*
AIKO: Yes. Alicia. I asked her to come and see you.
MARY: I had no idea. A missionary. I thought she was just some busybody.
AIKO: I like her. I think she has given up trying to convert the Japanese. She's just got used to being here.

INT. KABUKI STAGE. DAY
The musicians and Samisen players file into their positions.
AIKO: (*Voice over*) I told you I'd probably be away when the baby is born. I wanted someone to be there, if you needed anything.

INT. BOX IN THE KABUKI. DAY
MARY *looks at* AIKO, *troubled.*
MARY: Thank you.
    (*On-stage, the musicians begin playing and singing.*)

INT. KABUKI THEATRE. DAY
MARY's *point of view. The audience makes its casual way to its seats, talking, eating, thoroughly at home. Two women, one middle-aged, the other young, settle close by. The young woman's kimono is spectacularly gorgeous and contrasts with her companion's far drabber kimono.*
MARY: (*Voice over*) Isn't that beautiful?

INT. BOX IN THE KABUKI. DAY
AIKO *and* MARY *watch the young woman in the audience.*
AIKO: Yes, it means she is a courtesan, you can tell by these very gaudy colours in the kimono.
MARY: Oh.
    (*She watches, pensive, as the courtesan settles into her seat.*)

INT. KABUKI STAGE. DAY
The stage, where a dialogue is taking place between a woman and a small boy. The play is Chikamatsu's Shigenoi's Parting from her Son, *and in this scene,* SHIGENOI, *her face twisted into expressions*

43

*of extreme supplication and distress, clings to the boy and finally
enfolds him in the broad wings of her kimono.*
AIKO: (*Voice over*) All the actors are men, you know. Like in
    Shakespeare's time.

INT. BOX IN THE KABUKI. DAY
MARY's *face. She watches, absorbed.*
MARY: Why is she so unhappy?

INT. KABUKI STAGE. DAY
Now the boy is moving towards the catwalk to exit. SHIGENOI *has
her back to him, far away on the other side of the broad stage. As
the Narrator sings, off-screen, she turns, her face ravaged with grief,
to look over her shoulder at the departing child.*
AIKO: (*Voice over*) She has found her son but cannot keep him
    with her. He has agreed to go away and not disgrace her.
    But now she cannot bear to see him leave. It breaks her
    heart.

INT. BOX IN THE KABUKI. DAY
MARY *watches, moved and troubled.*

INT. KABUKI STAGE. DAY
The actor playing SHIGENOI *opens his mouth in a great, silent cry.
The musicians' accompaniment gradually fades to silence.*

EXT. VERANDA OF MARY'S HOUSE. EVENING
A piercing scream. MARY *rises from her chair, a hand clutching at
her abdomen.* MISAO *and* FUKUDA *appear, alarmed.* MARY *makes
one or two incoherent sounds and then totters forward.
Black screen.*

INT. LIVING-ROOM IN MARY'S HOUSE. DAY
*A baby, not more than a week old, to all intents and purposes
Japanese in appearance, lies peacefully in a bassinet. After a while,*
MARY's *hand reaches in to caress it, and a wider shot shows her,
pale but elated, propped up on her futon. She smiles.
From her point of view, a number of oranges are emptied from a
paper-bag into an empty fruit bowl. The donor, it then becomes*

apparent, is ALICIA BASSETT-HILL, *who stands, her expression a little constrained, looking down at* MARY.

MARY: Thank you.

ALICIA: Doctor Ikeda has asked me to have a little word with
    you.
    (MARY *looks up, immediately concerned.*)

MARY: The baby's all right, isn't he?

ALICIA: Of course he is, he's absolutely fine, strong as a horse.

MARY: Then what is it?
    (ALICIA *doesn't answer immediately.*)

ALICIA: It seems . . . well, it seems there were some
    complications during the delivery. To be perfectly honest
    my Japanese isn't quite good enough to be able to decipher
    all the details, it's not a field I know very much about, but
    the upshot of it is . . .
    (*She runs out of breath.* MARY *waits, painfully tense.*)
    It seems you won't be able to have any more children.
    (MARY *sinks back into the pillow. She looks almost relieved.*)

MARY: That's not so bad.
    (*She reaches out again, to tousle the baby's thick black hair.*)
    I'm sure he'll be more than enough.
    (*Tears begin to run down her cheeks.*
    ALICIA *watches for a moment, embarrassed, then leans forward
    to speak gently.*)

ALICIA: Have you thought of a name for him?
    (MARY *controls herself and tries to smile.*)

MARY: One of the nurses called him 'Taro'. That's from a story,
    isn't it?

ALICIA: That's right.

MARY: I thought I might call him Taro.

EXT. VERANDA OF MARY'S HOUSE. DAY

MARY *sits in her chair, feeding* TARO. *She looks down tenderly at the top of his head as it moves energetically to and fro.*

EXT. BANK OF THE SUMIDA RIVER. DAY

MARY *walks alone by the river.* TARO *is carried on her back in a sling, in the conventional Japanese arrangement. Passers-by look at her curiously.*
She stops to look down at the waters.

45

INT. LIVING-ROOM IN MARY'S HOUSE. NIGHT
MARY *wakes to hear* TARO's *insistent crying. She smiles to herself, emerges from between her quilts, turns the light on and moves towards the corner, where* TARO *is lying on a small quilt inside a specially constructed wooden playpen.* MARY *lifts him out and he stops crying at once.*

EXT. MARY'S HOUSE. DAY
It's raining. A delivery boy stands outside the front door, clutching an enormous parcel, which he hands over to MISAO *when she opens the door.*

INT. LIVING-ROOM. DAY
MARY's *chair has been moved indoors and put next to* TARO's *playpen. In the middle of the room,* MISAO *and* FUKUDA *are opening the parcel. They hand* MARY *a label, on which the word* MARY *(in English) and the address (in Japanese) are painted in black ink. The parcel itself is gradually unwrapped to reveal a giant red carp made of cloth on a wooden stand.* MISAO *explains to* MARY *in Japanese and* MARY *understands and tries haltingly to reply.*
MISAO: The red carp is the symbol of a boy.
MARY: Yes.
MISAO: Come. Come here.
      (MARY *gets up and goes over to* MISAO.)
      Put your hand in there.
      (*She guides* MARY's *hand to an opening under the fish's tail.* MARY *puts her hand in and draws out yards of material: heavy silk, bright patterns of flowers on a grey background.*)
      It's to make you a kimono.
MARY: Yes, I understand.

INT. KABUKI THEATRE. DAY
The courtesan, in her beautiful, brightly coloured kimono, takes her place in the stalls.

INT. LIVING-ROOM. DAY
MARY *runs her hand over the silk, her expression thoughtful. She speaks in English now.*
MARY: A kimono for a concubine.

(MISAO *finishes extracting the cloth from the fish. Out of the last fold drops a wallet in gold brocade. She picks it up and hands it to* MARY. MARY *opens it. It contains a number of brand-new hundred-yen notes.*)

INT. LIVING-ROOM IN ALICIA BASSETT-HILL'S HOUSE. DAY
ALICIA *has furnished her house with no regard whatsoever for Japanese custom: her living-room looks like a Victorian parlour, its heavy objects precariously sited on the soft matting.*
She serves MARY *and* AIKO *with traditional English tea, with milk and sugar to hand, as well as scones, buttered toast and home-made jam.* TARO *rolls contentedly around on the floor.*
MARY: I've been thinking of emigrating to America.
ALICIA: Surely not.
MARY: But I'm not sure they would consider me morally acceptable. And I don't know what it would be like for him.
AIKO: You must wait until Kurihama returns.
MARY: You think he will come and see me?
AIKO: The war will be over in a few weeks. Give him that time.
ALICIA: Don't you like it here?
MARY: It's not that. I just find it so difficult. I don't seem to be making any progress with the language. I can't get used to the food. Did it take you a long time to adjust?
ALICIA: I've always loved the country. I've been here twenty years without, as far as I know, making a single convert. I couldn't swear to it, because the Japanese are so polite, but I don't think they have much of a feel for Anglicanism. I can't say I mind all that much, though. As far as God is concerned, I suspect the effort is what matters the most.
AIKO: Why America and not your own country?
MARY: I couldn't go back there now: I'm not even sure they'd let me take Taro.
(*She looks up to find* ALICIA *offering her a plate of biscuits.*)
Shortbread? Where on earth did you find that?
ALICIA: It's home-made. Not a very demanding recipe.
(MARY *takes a biscuit.* AIKO *is watching her thoughtfully.*)
AIKO: It would not be fair to Kurihama to take away his child. Don't you think?

47

MARY: I suppose I should wait to find out what he intends, if anything.

AIKO: Next week is the Festival of the Dead.

MARY: Doesn't sound very cheerful.

AIKO: I must take you out one night to see it. You should understand some of our customs.

MARY: I don't like the idea of leaving him at night.

AIKO: You must bring him, it's good luck for children to greet the dead. And you should come also, Alicia.

ALICIA: I've tried very hard but I can't help being distressed by pagan rituals.

EXT. PRECINCTS OF THE ASAKUSA KANNON TEMPLE. NIGHT
The long narrow street approaching the temple is lit by thousands of lanterns and the occasional acetylene flare. Crowds of people shuffle towards the temple and the dominating sound is the clatter of wooden geta. The street is entirely lined with stalls selling lotus flowers, pottery, lanterns, straw mats, incense sticks, insects in cages, origami and innumerable other items for use in the ceremony.
AIKO and MARY (with TARO on her back) move slowly along with the procession. At a certain point, AIKO moves over to buy small offerings of rice and fruit on rice and straw mats. She gives one to MARY.

AIKO: We feed the dead when they return to visit us.

EXT. TEMPLE. NIGHT
The temple, with lanterns, towers ahead like something from some weird dream.

EXT. TEMPLE APPROACHES. NIGHT
Looking back from the temple, hundres of lanterns move towards it like a slow-flowing river.

EXT. TEMPLE. NIGHT
MARY and AIKO stand at the low barrier surrounding the temple and watch the ceremony within. There's a continuous tinkle as cash splashes into the offertory boxes. Inside, the brilliantly garbed priests move and intone. Everywhere, there are tiny offerings of food.
TARO is woken by the crash of the great temple gong. He reaches

forward to tug at MARY's *hair. She smiles and half turns to take his hand.*

EXT. BRIDGE. NIGHT
MARY *and* AIKO *stand on the bridge, looking down at the river. Its black water is ablaze with light. Hundreds of tiny wood and paper boats with miniature lanterns at their prow bob down towards the sea. It's a scene of unearthly beauty.*
AIKO: The boats are for the dead to sail back to their world for another year.
    (MARY *watches, entranced.*)

EXT. GARDEN OF MARY'S HOUSE. DAY
MARY *is in the garden, reading, with* TARO *nearby on his quilt.*
MISAO *is not far off, sewing. It's a scene of domestic tranquillity, established for a moment, before it's broken by the arrival of*
KENTARO KURIHAMA, *who appears very suddenly around the corner of the veranda.*
MISAO *jumps to her feet in total confusion and retreats into the house, bowing profoundly several times as she goes.* MARY *has got to her feet rather more slowly.*
He's in civilian (Japanese) clothes and moves towards her a little stiffly. MARY *holds out her hands to him and he takes them, looking at her for a moment, making no move to kiss her, until, suddenly and unexpectedly, he lunges forward to plant a quick kiss on her cheek.*
KENTARO: Mary.
MARY: You should have let me know you were coming.
KENTARO: I hoped you would be here.
MARY: Thank you for bringing me to Tokyo.
KENTARO: It was the right thing to do.
    (*He turns away from her to glance at* TARO, *who's looking interestedly up at him.*)
    Now.
MARY: He's hardly ever seen a man.
KENTARO: I shall be staying here for supper.
MARY: Of course.
    (KENTARO *moves over, his attention now fixed on the baby. He looks at him for a long time.* MARY *is almost afraid to break the silence.*)

49

Would you like to go inside?
(KENTARO *shows no signs of having heard. Eventually,
however, he reaches down and picks up the child.* MARY
gathers up the quilt and sets off towards the veranda.
KENTARO *follows, holding* TARO, *who seems quite fascinated
by him.*)

INT. LIVING-ROOM. DAY
MARY *moves into the living-room, followed by* KENTARO. *She's
about to put the quilt into the playpen when* KENTARO'*s voice
interrupts her.*
KENTARO: What is that?
MARY: He sleeps in it.
(KENTARO *calls out, immediately.* MARY, *not sure what's
going on, stands holding the quilt.*)
KENTARO: Misao San?
(MISAO *arrives quickly, flustered.* KENTARO *speaks to her in
Japanese, pointing to the playpen.*)
Take that thing away.
MISAO: Whatever you say.
KENTARO: Get rid of it.
(MISAO *picks the playpen up, a certain grim satisfaction in her
expression, and begins to move towards the door.*)
And another thing.
(*He takes* TARO'*s quilt from* MARY *and drops it over the side
of the playpen.*)
The child will sleep with you tonight.
MISAO: Yes.
(*She bows, smiling, and leaves the room.
He turns to* MARY, *switching back into English.*)
KENTARO: I don't like to see that.
MARY: When he learns to crawl, I thought it might reduce the
risk of accidents.
KENTARO: I don't want my son in a cage.
MARY: I see.
KENTARO: And now . . .
(KENTARO *breaks off, holding up the baby, apparently
considering how best to express himself.*)
. . . will you leave us alone for a while?
MARY: All right, if that's . . . what you want.

KENTARO: It is.
   (MARY, *a little hurt, starts to move to the door. Once there, she looks back, but* KENTARO *is already entirely absorbed in the baby and is no longer aware of her, so she hurries out.*)

EXT. GARDEN. EVENING
MARY *waits in the garden. The sun is setting. She paces up and down for a while, then stops to look at the silent house. Eventually, she sighs exasperatedly and moves decisively back towards the house, her expression fierce.*

INT. LIVING-ROOM. EVENING
MARY *sweeps into the living-room ready to remonstrate with* KENTARO, *but the protest dies on her lips when she sees him. He is down on one elbow on the floor, very skilfully tearing paper into animal shapes.* TARO *is lying on his stomach, watching* KENTARO, *entranced, one of his tiny fists closed round another paper animal.* KENTARO *looks up at* MARY *and gives one of his rare smiles.*
MARY: He's called Taro.
KENTARO: What?
MARY: Taro is the name I've chosen for him.
KENTARO: Ah.
   (KENTARO *stands another animal up in the row of them he's made, pointedly making no further comment. Then he picks the child up, looking at him closely and balancing him on one of his knees.*)
   He looks almost Japanese.
MARY: Almost?
KENTARO: Yes.
MARY: I'd say he looked entirely Japanese.
KENTARO: Would you?
   (*He looks at the baby again, his expression almost melancholy.*)
   Would you say that?

EXT. GARDEN. NIGHT
The house. Inside, MARY *cries out.*

INT. LIVING-ROOM. NIGHT
The lights are on. MARY *lies back between the quilts in* KENTARO's *arms.*

MARY: I worried about you all the time while the war was on.

KENTARO: If the death is an honourable death, there is nothing to fear.

MARY: We find it hard to think in those terms.

KENTARO: And yet you Christians believe in a life after death.

MARY: Not for non-Christians.

(KENTARO *laughs unexpectedly, and* MARY *smiles, in spite of herself.*)

In Mukden, everyone said you had no chance of winning the war.

KENTARO: It was good that we won, of course, but I am a little afraid, the Army, the Navy. I think now they may be given too much power.

MARY: I'd have thought you might have welcomed that.

KENTARO: No. The Army should serve the State, not control it.

(MARY *smiles at him again, languid, settling into the crook of his arm.*)

INT. LIVING-ROOM. NIGHT

Darkness.

MARY *starts up in response to the sound of* TARO, *crying in another room; she begins to scramble out of the quilt but* KENTARO *grips her firmly.*

KENTARO: Leave it.

MARY: No, I must . . .

KENTARO: Misao will go.

(*And, soon after he's spoken,* TARO's *crying stops: distant murmurs as* MISAO *attends to him. Eventually,* KENTARO *speaks very quietly.*)

You must not think you are the only one who can help the boy.

MARY: I'm his mother.

KENTARO: Oh, yes.

(*Silence.*)

MARY: You know I can never have another child.

KENTARO: The doctor told me.

MARY: Did he?

KENTARO: Of course.

MARY: I know you have other children.

KENTARO: I'm very sorry, believe me.

(*Silence.* MARY's *body relaxes. After a time,* KENTARO's
voice, barely a whisper.)
And now. Come. Again.
(*He draws her to him.*)

EXT. STREETS. DAY
MARY *is drawn along in a rickshaw through the streets of Tokyo.
Alongside, riding a bicycle of punishing design,* AIKO *rattles and
wobbles. She's wearing a curious, battered English tweed skirt
which, though less encumbering than a kimono, is far from ideal
bicycling wear.*

EXT. TSUSHIMAYA STORE AT UENO. DAY
MARY *descends from her rickshaw and* AIKO *brakes and dismounts
in front of an impressive two-storey building on the edge of Ueno
Park. The ground floor is decorated with red and white banners
hanging in strips and solid black and white banners, alternately; all
banners bearing (in white) the Tsushimaya symbol. There are no
windows, the low blank wooden walls of the upper storey are a pale
stripe between the dark grey slates of graceful roofs.*
MARY *follows* AIKO *towards one of the red and white banners
(which constitute the entrances) and pauses in the doorway,
preparing to hand in her shoes.*

INT. TSUSHIMAYA. DAY
*Inside, the shop is quite unlike a modern store. A limited supply of
goods are laid out on large, low, rectangular tables. On a huge,
partitionless expanse of tatami, delivery boys with shaven heads,
wearing grey tunics and leggings, hurry to and fro, but the shop
attendants, mostly ladies discreetly garbed in dark kimonos, are more
or less indistinguishable from the clientele.*
AIKO *bears down on one, however, and addresses her in Japanese.*
AIKO: Where is your department for Western clothes?
ATTENDANT: If you'd be so kind as to follow me.
   (*She sets off:* AIKO *and* MARY *follow her.*)
AIKO: What I need is a useful two-piece for bicycling.
ATTENDANT: We'll be happy to show you whatever we have.

INT. UPPER FLOOR AT TSUSHIMAYA. DAY
AIKO *and* MARY *arrive at the top of the stairs and follow the*

ATTENDANT *to a remote corner. Here there are a few unmistakably nineteenth-century gowns on headless dummies.* MARY *stops to look at them, her expression wavering between a frown and a smile.*

MARY: Good God, where did they excavate these from?

AIKO: My dear, these are the last word in fashion.

(*She turns to the* ATTENDANT, *speaking again in Japanese.*)
I don't think there's anything here, is there? What I need is cycling bloomers.

ATTENDANT: Please follow me.

(*There are a number of curtained-off alcoves round the perimeter of the room and the* ATTENDANT *leads them towards one of these.*)

INT. ALCOVE. DAY

The attendant directs AIKO *and* MARY *towards floor-cushions beside a low table: she opens a drawer in the table and presents* AIKO *with one of a number of large pattern books.*

ATTENDANT: Please be so kind as to look through this for a pattern.

(*As* AIKO *takes the book, the* ATTENDANT *opens another drawer to find an even larger book of material samples which she places on the table. Then she begins to withdraw from the alcove, bowing as she goes.*)
I shall be waiting just outside if you need me.

(MARY *is looking over* AIKO'S *shoulder as she turns the pages, fascinated by the patterns. The pages of the book show a range of nineties European styles.* MARY *stops the page turning by putting a hand on an entirely Victorian pattern.*)

MARY: They're about twenty years out of date.

AIKO: I know. I'm going to have to send off to New York in the end. I'm sorry, this is an absolute waste of time.

(*The* ATTENDANT *reappears with a tray; she's come to serve them tea.*

MARY, *meanwhile, has turned her attention to the book of material samples.*)

MARY: No, no, this is really fascinating.

INT. LIVING-ROOM IN MARY'S HOUSE. EVENING

MARY *is watching* KENTARO *eat his dinner, which he does with considerable noise and relish.*

A low brazier in the corner of the room indicates that the Tokyo
winter has now set in again.
MARY's expression is thoughtful.

MARY: How does your wife feel about this arrangement?
  (KENTARO *looks up at her, surprised. He stops eating for a*
  moment and considers: then resumes.)

KENTARO: There are things in Japan which as a rule are not
  discussed.

MARY: In Britain also; but then this is a state of affairs which
  has no . . . official equivalent in Britain.

KENTARO: Europeans, if I understand correctly, find it very
  difficult simply to *accept*: always questions, isn't that right?
  Here, what has to be is not questioned.

MARY: I see.
  (KENTARO *continues eating, fast and efficiently.*)
  I find it difficult not to know when to expect you.

KENTARO: I come when I can.

MARY: It's just something I haven't quite learned to accept.

KENTARO: You should live in the present: don't think about the
  past or worry for the future. Live the moment.

MARY: At least, when you're not here, I have Taro.
  (KENTARO *stops eating and looks uncomfortable for a moment.*
  Then he puts down the rice-bowl and looks directly at MARY.)

KENTARO: There are still many things in this country you have
  not understood. Sometimes hard decisions you may never
  understand. Or forgive.
  (MARY *looks at him, perplexed.*)

INT. LIVING-ROOM. DAWN
MARY *lies, still asleep, between the quilts.* KENTARO, *dressed now,*
moves quietly around the room, preparing to leave. Suddenly, she
starts, awakes, realizes what's happening.

MARY: Do you have to go?

KENTARO: Yes. Go back to sleep.

MARY: When will I see you?

KENTARO: I . . . have to go away for a time. To Korea.

MARY: For how long?

KENTARO: I don't know. But I will try to visit again before I
  leave.
  (MARY *scrambles up and goes to embrace him.*)

MARY: Yes. Do try.
> (KENTARO *kisses* MARY. *Then he holds her for a moment at arm's length, his expression, for once, weary and melancholy, studying her as if trying to imprint the image on his memory.*)

KENTARO: Goodbye.

INT. LIVING-ROOM. EVENING

MARY *looks up as* MISAO *puts her head round the door. Dialogue in Japanese, which in* MARY's *case is still very halting and tentative.*

MISAO: I think perhaps the little one should have some fresh air. He hasn't been out all day. Would you like me to take him out for a walk?

MARY: I don't think so.

MISAO: Just for five minutes. Down to the river.

MARY: All right.
> (MISAO *disappears and* MARY *looks thoughtfully at the door. Then she scrambles up from the floor and moves out into:*)

INT. FRONT HALL. EVENING

The front hall, where she's surprised to find MISAO *with* TARO (*now about six months old*) *already wrapped in warm clothes and wearing tiny knitted gloves. She helps* MISAO *to settle* TARO *in the sling on* MISAO's *back, after which* MISAO *wraps a* haori *coat around both of them.*

EXT. FRONT ENTRANCE. EVENING

Towards sunset. There's snow in the air.

MARY *follows* MISAO *and* TARO *out of the house, calling after them, again in Japanese.*

MARY: Just a moment.
> (MISAO *stops and half turns, all of a sudden with fear in her eyes.*
>
> MARY *moves to them to adjust* TARO's *woollen hat. As she's doing so, he manages to stretch out his gloved hand to touch her face. She leans forward to kiss him.*)

Don't be long.

MISAO: No.
> (TARO *looks over his shoulder at* MARY, *as* MISAO *hurries out of the gate.*)

INT. LIVING-ROOM. EVENING
It's almost dark: MARY, *looking worried, gets up and hurries out.*

INT. CORRIDOR. DAY
MARY *moves quickly down the corridor to:*

INT. KITCHEN. EVENING
The kitchen, where FUKUDA *looks up at her as she arrives, with big
startled eyes.*
MARY *strains to find the correct Japanese.*
MARY: Isn't Misao San back?
FUKUDA: No, Miss.
MARY: Where is she?
FUKUDA: I don't know, Miss.
    (FUKUDA *looks extremely shifty and uncomfortable. Suddenly,*
    MARY *is frightened. She shouts at* FUKUDA *in English.*)
MARY: What's she done to my baby?

EXT. HOUSE. EVENING
MARY *bursts out of the house, moving fast, not wearing a coat.*

EXT. BANK OF THE SUMIDA RIVER. NIGHT
It's quite dark now and MARY *stands, paralysed with uncertainty,
looking one way and then another, her breath rising on the cold night
air.*
MARY: Misao! Misao San!
    (*Suddenly, she catches sight of a woman with a baby passing
    by some way away. She runs towards her, calling as she goes.*)
    Misao! Is that you?
    (*As she draws alongside, the woman looks round, alarmed.*
    MARY *stops, realizing it isn't* MISAO; *and the woman hurries
    away.*)

INT. SERVANTS' QUARTERS IN MARY'S HOUSE. NIGHT
FUKUDA *looks up apprehensively as* MARY *bursts into the room,
shouting in broken Japanese.*
MARY: The police! Go . . . police!
    (FUKUDA *scrambles to her feet.*)

57

EXT. MARY'S HOUSE. NIGHT
MARY *stands in the doorway, her arms wrapped round her, grey and shivering.*

INT. KABUKI STAGE. DAY
SHIGENOI *turns, ravaged with grief, to watch her son vanish.*

EXT. MARY'S HOUSE. NIGHT
MARY *starts forward as* FUKUDA *appears with two uniformed policemen and, bringing up the rear,* DOCTOR IKEDA. MARY *grabs hold of* FUKUDA, *speaks to her urgently in Japanese.*
MARY: Now go to the Hotel Okatsu. Ask the Baroness Onnodera to come.
　　(DOCTOR IKEDA *intervenes, speaking English.*)
IKEDA: She is away in Osaka.
MARY: Then we must send for Count Kurihama.
IKEDA: It is too late in the night.
MARY: It doesn't matter.
IKEDA: It's very late. Let me give you something to help you sleep.
　　(*Suddenly* MARY *glares at him suspiciously.*)
MARY: What are you doing here?
IKEDA: Fukuda San told me. You must be calm.
MARY: Calm? Where's my baby?
IKEDA: Come inside. I will help you to explain everything to the police.

INT. LIVING-ROOM. NIGHT
MARY *wakes with a start, remembers at once, groans in anguish.*

EXT. BANK OF THE SUMIDA RIVER. DAWN
As dawn breaks, MARY *wanders hopelessly to and fro.*

INT. KABUKI STAGE. DAY
The actor playing SHIGENOI *opens his mouth in a great silent cry.*

INT. ANTE-ROOM AT THE BRITISH EMBASSY. DAY
MARY *and* ALICIA *wait in a tense silence. Eventually, the door*

opens and the First Secretary arrives, an Englishman, his manner smooth and composed. MARY springs to her feet.

SECRETARY: Please sit down.

(MARY takes no notice.)

MARY: Well?

SECRETARY: Sir Claude regrets he is unable to see you, he is receiving a trade delegation.

ALICIA: Is there no way you can help?

SECRETARY: If, in fact, a crime has been committed, the matter is in the hands of the police. If, on the other hand, the child has been removed by its father . . .

(MARY looks at him, her expression fierce.)

. . . the matter is completely outside our jurisdiction, and on the face of it the father would seem to be completely within his legal rights.

MARY: You mean he's allowed to steal my baby?

SECRETARY: If it is his child, under Japanese law he has absolute authority to do so.

MARY: Is that all you're going to say?

ALICIA: I think we should leave, Mary.

MARY: You aren't going to give me any help at all?

SECRETARY: I really am most sympathetic . . .

MARY: No, you're not, you're a mealy-mouthed coward.

ALICIA: Come along, Mary.

INT. RECEPTION AREA IN THE BRITISH EMBASSY. DAY

ALICIA leads MARY, who is sobbing bitterly, across the reception area.

ALICIA: I think you should come and stay with me for a few days.

(MARY's response is almost violent.)

MARY: No. Suppose they bring him back.

INT. LIVING-ROOM IN MARY'S HOUSE. NIGHT

MARY sits on her calves, Japanese fashion, waiting. Eventually, she springs to her feet.

EXT. STREETS. NIGHT

The back of the ricksaw-man's head as he runs through the freezing night.

EXT. BRITISH AMBASSADOR'S RESIDENCE. NIGHT

SIR CLAUDE *is wishing goodnight to the last of his guests. As they disappear, he stands for a moment, playing with his moustache, enjoying the crisp night air. He's startled by* MARY's *voice.*

MARY: (*Off-screen*) Sir Claude.

SIR CLAUDE: Who is it?

> (MARY *steps into the light from the shadow of the wall, under which she's been waiting.*)

MARY: I don't know if you remember me. Mary Collingsworth.

SIR CLAUDE: Ah, Mrs Collingsworth, yes, of course.

MARY: I'm sorry to approach you like this, I couldn't think how else to get to speak to you.

> (SIR CLAUDE *has recovered from his shock and assumed a wary, official manner.*)

SIR CLAUDE: Through the usual channels, I imagine.

MARY: It's too urgent for the usual channels, my baby's been kidnapped.

SIR CLAUDE: I do know something of the circumstances of this. I'm not sure 'kidnapped' is the appropriate term.

MARY: It's what's happened.

SIR CLAUDE: I understand there is a possibility the child might simply have been reclaimed by its father.

MARY: And they tell me that's not against the law.

SIR CLAUDE: There really is nothing to be done. Indeed, if you were to succeed in finding him and you took him back, then *you* would be committing an offence; a crime, if you attempted to take him out of the country.

MARY: But he's my baby, what can I do?

SIR CLAUDE: Isn't that a question you should have asked yourself last year in Manchuria?

MARY: What's the use of saying a thing like that? You want me to regret having my child?

> (*Silence.* SIR CLAUDE *is momentarily at a loss.*)

SIR CLAUDE: The only thing I can advise is that you apply to the Consul for repatriation. I don't say it would automatically be granted, but I think I could undertake to ease the way for you.

MARY: How can I leave this country when I know my child is somewhere in it?

SIR CLAUDE: I don't believe there's any other way I can help
you.
(*He turns abruptly and begins to move back into the house.
Then he stops, turns back and adds as an afterthought:*)
You've been a great disappointment to me, Mrs
Collingsworth.
(*He's gone, leaving* MARY *shivering on the doorstep.*)

INT. LIVING-ROOM IN MARY'S HOUSE. NIGHT
MARY *sits up between her quilts. She listens intently for a moment.
From somewhere in the house, scarcely audible, the sound of
whispered voices.*

INT. SERVANTS' QUARTERS. NIGHT
MARY *bursts into the room.* MISAO *is on her knees, packing clothes
into a wicker basket, watched by* FUKUDA. *She looks up, terrified.*
MARY *moves over to her and grabs her. She wriggles free and makes
a dash for the doorway with* MARY *in hot pursuit.*

INT. KITCHEN/CORRIDOR. NIGHT
MARY *catches* MISAO *in the hall. They grapple silently for a
moment, swaying to and fro, indirectly lit. Then* MISAO *topples over
and* MARY *dives on top of her, beginning to shout at her in a
mixture of Japanese and English.*
MARY: Where is he? Where's my child? What have you done
with him? Where's my baby? Where is he? Where?
(*She is banging* MISAO's *head against the matting. Eventually,*
FUKUDA *succeeds in dragging her off* MISAO, *and while* MARY
struggles with her, MISAO *makes good her escape, scuttling out
of the door and away, as* MARY *yells after her in Japanese.*)
Where is he?

EXT. MARY'S HOUSE. NIGHT
MISAO *flees from the house and disappears through the gate.*

INT. AIKO'S ROOM IN THE OKATSU HOTEL. DAY
MARY *sits listening to* AIKO, *an expression of hopelessness on her
face.*
AIKO: You see, it's considered much better for a child to be
brought up as what we call a *yoshi*, an adopted son in a

good family, than to be brought up by a single woman. The system works like this: the boy goes into a family where there is no son. If there is a daughter, he will eventually marry her. There are many families who would be more than happy to adopt a Kurihama. If he had been white, of course, they would have let you keep him.

(*Silence. Eventually,* MARY *speaks in a very small, exhausted voice.*)

MARY: So when can I see him?

AIKO: It's not usual for the child to maintain any contact with his natural parent. You must ask Kurihama.

MARY: He's in Korea, and I don't suppose I shall ever see him again, any more than I'll see Taro . . . or whatever they decide to call him.

(MARY *breaks down, sobbing helplessly. After a time,* AIKO *comes over, kneels down beside her and takes her in her arms. She strokes her hair as* MARY *buries her face in* AIKO's *shoulder, her body racked with sobs.*)

EXT. BANK OF THE SUMIDA RIVER. NIGHT. 1906
It is snowing. MARY, *who is not even wearing a coat, stares down at the fast-flowing water. She moves to the very edge of the riverbank. She leans towards the water, her face ashen.*

INT. KABUKI STAGE. DAY
As before: the actor's silent cry.

EXT. BANK OF THE SUMIDA RIVER. NIGHT
MARY *straightens up. She suddenly looks determined and defiant. She turns away from the river, shivering, and hurries off.*

EXT. OKATSU HOTEL. DAY
MARY *descends from a rickshaw outside the shabby hotel where* AIKO *lives. Her luggage consists of a couple of small suitcases.*

INT. MARY'S ROOM IN THE HOTEL. DAY
MARY's *dingy room is much the same as* AIKO's: *a little smaller and even less recently decorated.*
MARY *finishes unpacking and looks around, still putting a brave*

face on it. Next door, through the thin walls, she hears somebody
coughing.
A light tap on the door and AIKO *enters, her expression concerned.*
AIKO: Are you sure this is wise?
MARY: I thought you were in favour of female emancipation.
AIKO: Yes, but to come here . . .
MARY: I can't stay in that house.
AIKO: I suppose I can understand that.
MARY: And I'm not going to accept any more of his money.
AIKO: Then how will you live?
MARY: I don't know.
    (*She does her best to smile.*)
    Surely we can think of something.

THREE

EXT. PRECINCTS OF THE ASAKUSA TEMPLE. NIGHT
As before, MARY and AIKO move through the crowds as they
approach the temple amid a sea of bobbing lanterns. TARO on
MARY's back, in his sling, reaches out to touch her face and she
half-turns, smiling.
As MARY's voice continues, a series of images from the Festival of
the Dead.
MARY: (*Voice over*) I see the infant's ghost being borne through
   just such a peaceful throng as this, in just such a lukewarm,
   luminous night, peeping over the mother's shoulder, softly
   clinging at her neck with tiny hands. Somewhere among
   this multitude she is – the mother. She will feel again
   tonight the faint touch of little hands, yet will not turn her
   head to look and laugh, as in other days.

INT. MARY'S ROOM IN THE OKATSU HOTEL. EVENING
MARY is in bed. The book by Lafcadio Hearn, which she's been
reading, slips from her hands. Her body shakes with sobs.
She climbs out of bed. In a corner, her suitcases are piled in a heap.
She moves the top suitcase and opens the one below. It contains all
Taro's clothes. MARY looks for a moment, then chooses a tiny wool
sleeping-suit. She buries her face in it, trying to recapture some
essence of the child.

EXT. TSUSHIMAYA STORE AT UENO. DAY
MARY and AIKO approach the store. MARY looks extremely
apprehensive. AIKO smiles at her encouragingly.
AIKO: Courage.
   (*They set off into the store.*)

INT. HIROSHI TSUSHIMA'S OFFICE. DAY
The plain, elegant private office of MR HIROSHI TSUSHIMA, the
proprietor of the shop. There are a few concessions to Westernization
– an ebony desk, for example, and three chairs for AIKO, MARY
and MR TSUSHIMA himself – but the screens, the tatami, the
kakemono *representing a waterfall, are all quintessentially Japanese.*

Tea has been served, and now TSUSHIMA *is frowning across his desk at* AIKO, *his expression, as often, deeply sceptical. He's a small bespectacled man of about sixty, wearing a Western business suit. Dialogue in Japanese.*

TSUSHIMA: Our sales figures are excellent.

AIKO: If you were the only shop in Tokyo selling modern Western clothes, I guarantee they would improve.

TSUSHIMA: Could she design them herself?

(AIKO *hesitates for a second;* MARY'*s looking quite concerned.*)

AIKO: Well . . .

TSUSHIMA: It would obviously be quite uneconomic to import them.

AIKO: Of course she could, she's always made all her own clothes.

TSUSHIMA: I see.

AIKO: And I think there's no doubt an English saleslady would be a point of considerable interest to your customers.

TSUSHIMA: There is always the difficulty of how they would communicate with her.

MARY: I understand most of what is said . . . and I'm trying to learn to speak better Japanese.

(TSUSHIMA *looks at* MARY *for a moment, surprised. Then he speaks directly to* MARY.)

TSUSHIMA: Would you be so kind as to explain to me how you would go about reforming my business? You may speak in English, I think I will be able to follow.

(MARY *hesitates for a second, then plunges in, relieved to be allowed to speak English.*)

MARY: First, I would need to spend some time preparing a collection. I'd want to study all the latest fashion magazines from Europe – don't forget it's more than three years since I left – and use them as a starting-point, making whatever modifications may be necessary, taking into account that there are certain basic differences in the Japanese figure. Then I would need to work with a team; above all, I'd have to have a very good cutter. We could be ready in, let's say, three months . . .

(TSUSHIMA *frowns.*)

. . . two months . . .

(*His expression lightens.*)

66

. . . and you could donate all your present stock to a
museum.

(TSUSHIMA *doesn't understand this. He turns interrogatively to*
AIKO, *speaking in Japanese.*)

TSUSHIMA: What was that?

AIKO: English sense of humour.

TSUSHIMA: Ah.

(MARY *continues in English, pressing her point.*)

MARY: It's true, though, if you wanted to find clothes like you
have here in London or Edinburgh, you'd need to go to a
theatrical costumier.

(TSUSHIMA *turns to* AIKO *again.*)

TSUSHIMA: What did she say?

(AIKO *explains.* TSUSHIMA *receives the explanation in silence.*
He ponders for a moment. It's some time before he speaks.)

I normally start my salesladies off at fifty yen a month.

AIKO: Then you won't mind giving Mackenzie San a hundred,
will you?

(TSUSHIMA *contemplates* AIKO *bleakly for a moment.*)

TSUSHIMA: Eighty.

(MARY *intervenes quickly in Japanese.*)

MARY: I accept with thanks.

(TSUSHIMA *nods, then rings a little silver bell on his desk.*
Presently a male secretary appears.)

TSUSHIMA: Hinobe.

(*The secretary bows and exits.*
Silence.
TSUSHIMA *bestows on* MARY *a fraction of a smile, then he*
speaks.)

Can you start on Sunday?

MARY: Tomorrow, if you like.

TSUSHIMA: Sunday will do. We gather at eight fifteen.

(*There's a discreet tap at the door and* HINOBE *appears, a*
small hunched man of about fifty. HINOBE *bows in the*
doorway and advances a tentative step into the room.)

Ah, Hinobe, this is your new assistant.

(HINOBE's *eyes narrow momentarily. Then he turns on* MARY
a look of undisguised hatred, which vanishes immediately as he
bows to her.)

67

INT. TRAM. DAY
MARY *stands in a crowded tram, swaying as it clatters across Tokyo.*
She's looking wistfully at a baby in a sling on its mother's back. She
reaches out a finger and the child's tiny hand closes around it.

EXT. STAFF ENTRANCE AT TSUSHIMAYA. DAY
MARY *joins the jostling mass of employees handing in their shoes at*
the staff entrance. Women in dark kimonos, delivery boys in grey
uniforms, salesmen in Western business suits, doormen resplendent in
gold-braided navy-blue uniforms with peaked cap, girl-workers in
purple blouses, shoe-finders in black collarless tunics, buttoned to the
neck. A good many of them glance at her curiously.

INT. TSUSHIMAYA. DAY
The top floor of Tsushimaya contains several groups of employees,
each group standing in formation, being addressed by its head of
department. MARY *is part of the group respectfully listening to*
HINOBE.
HINOBE: Mrs Yamanuchi, would you step forward, please?
       (MRS YAMANUCHI, *a nervous-looking middle-aged woman,*
       does so.)
       Would you show us how you greet a customer?
MRS YAMANUCHI: Welcome to Tsushimaya, is there any way in
       which I might be of assistance to you?
       (*She looks apprehensively at* HINOBE, *who turns, his*
       expression neutral, to the group.)
HINOBE: Any comments?
       (*A keen-looking young woman,* MISS ARIMA, *puts her hand*
       up.)
       Arima San?
MISS ARIMA: I'm not sure it was sincere enough.
HINOBE: There is some justice in this, you must make the
       customer feel it is genuinely an honour to serve her.
MRS YAMANUCHI: Yes, Mr Hinobe.
       (*During this last exchange, a lively young woman standing near*
       MARY *catches her eye, her expression unmistakably amused.*
       This is MINAGAWA SAN. MARY *half-smiles in response.*)

INT. CUTTING-ROOM. DAY
The staff in the cutting-room are MINAGAWA SAN *and a much older*

woman, MRS KATSURA, *who at the moment is looking dubiously at various patterns which* MARY *has spread out for them. After a while,* MARY *speaks in her halting Japanese.*

MARY: Can you understand them? Do you think you'll be able to make any sense of them?

(MRS KATSURA *shakes her head, sighing lugubriously.*)

KATSURA: I don't know.

MINAGAWA: I'm sure we will.

INT. WORKROOM. DAY

MINAGAWA SAN *shows* MARY *around the sewing-room, a cramped attic space, with eight primitive sewing machines clattering away.* MINAGAWA SAN *points out various aspects of the room, her voice inaudible behind the sewing machines.*

INT. CHANGING-ROOM. DAY

MARY *stands watching as two salesgirls take the measurements of a customer, who stands in the centre of the room wearing an under-kimono. After a time, the salesgirl who is writing down the measurements hands the completed list to* MINAGAWA SAN, *who beckons to* MARY *to follow her.*

INT. FITTING-ROOM. DAY

MINAGAWA SAN *leads* MARY *into a room containing a score or so of adustable wire dressmaker's shapes. She selects one and begins altering the proportions in accordance with the list of measurements in her hand.*

INT. TSUSHIMAYA. DAY

MARY *stands on duty in her department, discreetly massaging the back of an aching thigh. At a certain point she turns to find* HINOBE *staring at her, his expression frankly hostile. He looks away immediately.*

INT. TRAM. NIGHT

It's dark outside. MARY *sways to and fro in the crowded tram, scarcely able to keep her eyes open.*

INT. MARY'S ROOM IN THE OKATSU HOTEL. EVENING

MARY *sits at her desk, massaging her calves. Beside her, on the desk, there's an open envelope. It contains a large number of hundred-yen notes.*

There's a knock at the door and AIKO *enters the room.*

AIKO: How was it?

MARY: Exhausting.

AIKO: I was afraid it might be.

MARY: Ten hours a day, three days off a month, four days holiday a year, I'm a girl from the leisured classes, I'm not sure I can manage it.

(*She smiles wearily.*)

AIKO: Of course you can.

MARY: And here's Kentaro sending me the equivalent of about five years' salary.

(MARY *flourishes the envelope.*)

AIKO: I see.

MARY: You know how to get in touch with him . . .

AIKO: No, I . . .

MARY: Yes, you do. I want you to see this is returned to him: ask him to use it to open a bank account for Taro.

AIKO: Are you sure?

MARY: Don't ask: just do it.

AIKO: All right.

(*She takes the money from* MARY.)

Shall we have some supper?

MARY: I'm too tired to eat.

(AIKO *smiles at her sympathetically.*)

And another thing. I can't afford to live here much longer. I have to find a house.

AIKO: Leave it to me.

EXT. MARY'S HOUSE AT OTSUKA. NIGHT

A tiny house in a dilapidated wooden terrace in an unfashionable quarter of northern Tokyo.

The sky is just beginning to lighten.

INT. MARY'S BEDROOM. NIGHT

MARY'*s bedroom is the single upstairs room over a living-room and a maid's room. She moves around getting ready for the day; she looks exhausted.*

70

*A table in the corner of the room has been arranged as a kind of
shrine to* TARO: *his clothes, his shoes, his toys.*

INT. TRAM. DAY
In the crowded tram, MARY *is juggling with pattern-books and a
pencil, with which she jots notes in the margin. At a certain point the
jolting of the tram causes her to drop one of the books. It's picked up
by a young man of about nineteen,* AKIRA SUZUKI, *who is himself
carrying enough books to make it fairly clear he's a student. He
hands it back to her and she thanks him in Japanese.*
MARY: Thank you.
    (*To her surprise,* SUZUKI *answers, with some difficulty, but
    understandably, in English.*)
SUZUKI: Please don't mention it.
    (*She smiles at him uncertainly, then resumes her work on the
    pattern-book.*)

INT. HIROSHI TSUSHIMA'S OFFICE. DAY
MR TSUSHIMA *has a copy of the house magazine which he appears
to be studying for the moment.* MARY *waits, standing just inside the
door. Eventually he looks up at her, speaking in Japanese.*
TSUSHIMA: Your clothes are going to be ready by the first of
    May?
MARY: Yes, I hope so.
TSUSHIMA: So do I, because as you can see we've announced it
    in our company magazine.
    (*He shows her the magazine, in which she's surprised to see a
    photograph of herself over several columns of print.*)
    I've sent out a great many invitations as well: I expect
    you've planned some kind of a show for us.
MARY: A show?
TSUSHIMA: Isn't that what they call it?
    (*He smiles at* MARY, *thinly.*)
    Thank you.
MARY: Thank you, sir.
    (*She bows to him and leaves the room, frowning.*)

INT. CUTTING-ROOM. DAY
The cutting-room has completely lost its air of neatness and calm.

Now, it's chaos: bales of cloth, cut-out pieces of fabric, scraps of material, patterns, all jumbled together.
MINAGAWA SAN *is working in a corner, but in the centre of the room, slumped at a table,* MRS KATSURA *stares hopelessly at a pattern.* MARY *reacts instantly, addressing her in Japanese.*
MARY: What's the matter?
KATSURA: I can't understand the pattern.
    (MARY *goes to look over her shoulder.*)
MARY: It's quite simple. What can't you understand?
KATSURA: Any of it, Mackenzie San.
    (KATSURA's *lip begins to tremble.*)
MARY: Well, leave it. Find one you can understand.

INT. WORKROOM. DAY
The machines rattle away. MARY *moves from one to the other, inspecting the work.*
Atmosphere of purposeful calm.

INT. CUTTING-ROOM. NIGHT
MARY's *working in* MRS KATSURA's *place, squinting in the dim light cast by the gas-lamp (electric light is confined to the public areas of the store).* MINAGAWA *is still in her corner, working swiftly and efficiently.*
MARY *consults her watch, which is lying on the table covered by the flimsy pattern paper. It's after midnight. She looks over at* MINAGAWA *and speaks in Japanese.*
MARY: You'd better go.
MINAGAWA: It's all right.
MARY: No.
    (MINAGAWA *yawns and stretches.*)
MINAGAWA: What about you?
MARY: I'm staying.
MINAGAWA: Then I'll stay with you.

INT. NOODLE SHOP. DAY
MARY *eats greedily at a rough table in a workman's café.* AIKO *sits opposite her. Dialogue in English.*
AIKO: You mean they walk up and down wearing the clothes?
MARY: That's right, they demonstrate them. It's a French idea.
    I read about it in a magazine, just before I left home.

AIKO: And where are you going to find these . . .
    demonstrators?
MARY: The girls from the workroom.
    (*Silence.* AIKO *considers.*)
AIKO: There's never been anything like this in Japan before.
    How am I supposed to convince Tsushima to agree to it?
MARY: He said he wanted a show.

INT. TRAM. NIGHT
It's raining. MARY *scrambles on to the tram, and stands, jammed in
the crowd, struggling to keep her eyes open. Eventually, however,
she becomes aware of the presence of* AKIRA SUZUKI, *who's
standing not far off, staring at her. She frowns for a second, trying
to place him. Then, as she succeeds, he smiles and inclines his head
to her.* MARY *responds minimally and then begins to look rather
alarmed as he starts to ease his way through the crowd between
them. When he's finally arrived in the space next to her, he speaks in
his very approximate English.*
SUZUKI: Good morning.
MARY: Hello.
SUZUKI: Good day.
MARY: Yes.
    (*She waits, as* SUZUKI *struggles for the words.*)
SUZUKI: You give me lessons . . . English . . .
MARY: What?
SUZUKI: I want English lessons.
MARY: Oh, I see.
SUZUKI: I pay you.
MARY: I'm afraid I'm too busy.
SUZUKI: Uh?
MARY: I don't have time just now.
SUZUKI: I do not . . . understand . . .
    (MARY *sighs, a little exasperated, and then speaks to him
    bluntly, in Japanese.*)
MARY: Too much work.
SUZUKI: Oh, excuse me.
    (MARY *nods, softening a little, half smiling as he begins to
    back away from her.*)

73

INT. CUTTING-ROOM. NIGHT
MARY *works on in the deserted office. She's scribbling figures on a piece of paper. At a certain point, her eyes close and she falls asleep, her chin resting in the palm of her hand.*

INT. FITTING-ROOM. NIGHT
The wire dummies are all wearing MARY's *clothes for the show. She moves among them, inspecting each one, straightening a lapel, brushing off fluff, making minute adjustments. As she does so, the sound of an expectant crowd begins to rise.*

INT. TSUSHIMAYA. DAY
The milling crowd of customers.
Rows of cushions set out on the floor.
MARY, *tense, black circles under her eyes, watches them nervously.*
HINOBE, *disapproval personified, stares at her.*
AIKO *and* ALICIA BASSETT-HILL *are in the crowd, and the latter waves affectionately at* MARY, *who responds with a rather tight smile.*
There's another woman, a Japanese, standing a little apart, looking at MARY, *who eventually notices her, registers her interest and then looks away. The woman, who, as we shall subsequently discover, is the* COUNTESS KURIHAMA, *continues to stare at her.*

INT. CHANGING-ROOM. DAY
The girls from the workroom, now transformed into models, are getting ready for the show, helping each other, giggling, exhilarated.
MARY *passes among them, sternly inspecting those who are ready.*

INT. TSUSHIMAYA. DAY
The audience is now settled in rows on the floor. Photographic equipment is in place, arranged behind the audience.
MARY *lurks by the curtain which leads off to the changing-rooms.*
TSUSHIMA *himself is addressing the audience in Japanese.*
TSUSHIMA: These will be the most up-to-date European ladies' clothes to be found anywhere in Japan. Exclusively designed for us by our *couturière* from England . . .
    (MARY *mutters under her breath.*)
MARY: Scotland.
TSUSHIMA: . . . and not obtainable anywhere except at

Tsushimaya, we proudly present to you, our most
distinguished customers, the Edinburgh Collection.
(TSUSHIMA *gestures to* MARY, *who pulls back the curtain and
stands back as the models emerge. They take their positions and
turn gracefully, their movements accompanied by the store's
youth band, playing with more enthusiasm than skill.
It's hard to assess the reaction of the public.*
AIKO *and* ALICIA *begin to applaud and it's taken up by one or
two of the others, but the applause never rises above a polite
ripple.*
HINOBE *watches, his features set in a permanent sneer.*
MARY *can't take any more after a while and slips away into
the changing-room.*)

INT. CHANGING-ROOM. DAY
MARY *sits in the changing-room, her face buried in her hands, a
picture of exhaustion and desolation. Then the models file into the
room and she's on her feet immediately, helping them to change,
alongside* MINAGAWA SAN *who's led them back into the changing-
room. The models change with frenzied but well-organized haste.*

INT. TSUSHIMAYA. DAY
*The show draws to a close. The models bow and disappear, herded
away by* MINAGAWA SAN.
TSUSHIMA, *who's been watching impassively, rises to his feet to say
a few words.*
TSUSHIMA: Thank you very much, ladies, for your patience and
    attention. If any of you would like to make orders, my
    Head of Department, Mr Hinobe, over there, would be
    delighted to take them.
    (HINOBE *bows and smiles, but in the audience no one has
    moved. People begin slowly rising to their feet but nobody
    approaches* HINOBE. *He looks at* MARY, *his eyes shining with
    malicious satisfaction. Then, suddenly, he turns away, his
    expression changing.
    Another angle explains why. Dozens of women are bearing
    down on* HINOBE. *There's a last glimpse of his astonished face
    before he's engulfed in customers.*
    TSUSHIMA *looks at* MARY *and permits himself the smallest of*

*frosty smiles before departing, attended by his secretaries and
personal staff.*
AIKO *and* ALICIA *join* MARY.)
ALICIA: Well done, it does look like an enormous success.
MARY: Do you think so?
ALICIA: Well, look at them.
AIKO: I'm going to make some orders.
  (*She hurries off to join the gesticulating crowd of customers.*
  ALICIA *turns back to* MARY.)
ALICIA: Are they really wearing things like that back home?
  (MARY'*s first instinct is indignation, then she relaxes and
  smiles.*)
MARY: Yes. Yes, they are.
  (*As she finishes speaking, she once again becomes aware of the*
  COUNTESS KURIHAMA *who, isolated now in the body of the
  room, is looking at her intently: as she returns the* COUNTESS'*s
  stare, the latter turns and sets off for the staircase down to the
  ground floor.* MARY *watches her go, puzzled.*)

INT. LIVING-ROOM IN ALICIA BASSETT-HILL'S HOUSE. DAY
ALICIA *has been entertaining* MARY *and* AIKO *for tea, as well as
her new American neighbours –* BOB *and* EMMA LOU DALE.
*He's a tall, bespectacled, serious-looking young man in his late
twenties, while she is small, intense in manner, several months
pregnant, and a couple of years younger than her husband.*
MARY: We sold every single piece in the collection and took
  orders for more than twice as much again.
BOB: You did?
MARY: And the orders have been pouring in ever since. Hinobe
  is furious. He's the Head of our Department.
EMMA LOU: Why should he be furious?
MARY: He disapproves on principle.
BOB: It's certainly not an easy country to do business in. My
  bank, the Kansas and Midwest Warranty Trust, has put
  out some real generous loan schemes, but the Japanese
  don't seem to like the idea of borrowing. Leastways, they
  don't like the idea of borrowing dollars.
AIKO: We don't much care for foreign money, we don't really
  understand it.
BOB: Money's money.

ALICIA: I expect they're keener on dollars than they are on
    Anglicanism.
    (*She smiles, gets up and crosses to her incongruously heavy
    sideboard.*)
    Well now, I don't think it's too early for a glass of sherry,
    do you?
BOB: Oh, thank you, we don't.
ALICIA: Probably just as well, it's awfully hard to come by.
BOB: We take no alcohol at all.
ALICIA: Oh, I see.
    (ALICIA *pours sherry for herself, for* MARY *and for* AIKO.
    MARY *meanwhile has been looking at* EMMA LOU.)
MARY: When is it due?
EMMA LOU: Oh, September, I guess. I never expected I would
    have a child who was born in Japan. You can't imagine
    what a strange idea that is.
MARY: No.
    (*She looks away and* AIKO *comes to the rescue.*)
AIKO: Is this your first?
EMMA LOU: Oh, no, we have two boys already.
ALICIA: Are you sure you won't change your mind?
    (EMMA LOU *looks up at her, speaks a touch defiantly.*)
EMMA LOU: Why, yes, I will, thank you.
    (EMMA LOU *takes a glass of sherry:* BOB *watches her grimly.*
    ALICIA *has to nudge* MARY *to draw her attention back to the
    sherry she's offering her.*)

INT. TRAM. DAY
This time, MARY *has managed to find a seat, and from it, she
notices* AKIRA SUZUKI, *standing not far off. She watches him for a
while, considering: then, when he looks over in her direction, she
beckons him over. He hesitates, she beckons again; and he begins to
push through the crowd towards her. When he arrives next to her,
she addresses him in English.*
MARY: Why do you want to learn English?
SUZUKI: Excuse me?
MARY: English. You want to learn English. Why?
SUZUKI: I am student.
MARY: Student of English?
SUZUKI: Yes.

MARY: I see.

SUZUKI: I can pay.

MARY: You can pay me with Japanese lessons.

(SUZUKI *doesn't seem to have grasped this so she repeats the
remark in Japanese.* SUZUKI's *expression clears.*)

SUZUKI: Ah, yes.

MARY: Shall we say Tuesdays?

SUZUKI: Yes.

MARY: Eight o'clock.

SUZUKI: Yes.

(MARY *finds a card in her bag and gives it to him.*)

MARY: There's the address.

(SUZUKI *takes the card and bows.*)

SUZUKI: I am Suzuki Akira.

MARY: See you on Tuesday.

(SUZUKI *bows again and backs away from her.
This discussion has been watched with the greatest of interest by
the other passengers.*)

INT. HIROSHI TSUSHIMA'S OFFICE. DAY

MARY *stands, waiting, in* TSUSHIMA's *office while he, apparently
abstracted, picks at his teeth. Eventually, he seems to come to and
addresses her brusquely in Japanese.*

TSUSHIMA: Please sit down.

(MARY *does so, pleasantly surprised. She waits.*)

I understand you had a visit from a gentleman from
Beniya.

MARY: What? Oh, yes, that's right.

TSUSHIMA: What did he want?

MARY: To offer me a job.

TSUSHIMA: I see.

MARY: I told him I was very happy here.

(*Ghost of a smile from* TSUSHIMA. *He reflects for a moment.*)

TSUSHIMA: I think we made a mistake when we fixed your
salary.

MARY: Oh?

TSUSHIMA: I believe we should have said a hundred yen a
month, after all.

MARY: Thank you.

TSUSHIMA: You may go.

78

INT. LIVING-ROOM IN MARY'S HOUSE. NIGHT
*The door is open on to the minuscule area at the back of the house to
take advantage of what breeze there is.* MARY *and* SUZUKI *are
sitting on the floor, armed with notebooks and pencils.*
MARY *finishes making a note and then looks up and speaks to*
SUZUKI *in English.*
MARY: Right now, Mr Suzuki, we're going to see if we can
    frame a question correctly. Concentrate if you will on the
    word order.
    (SUZUKI *looks up at her for a moment, his liquid eyes
    troubled.*)
SUZUKI: Will you marry me?
MARY: Very good. Absolutely correct. Now shall we try
    something a little more complicated?
    (SUZUKI *frowns.*)
SUZUKI: No, I mean, Miss Mackenzie, I mean, will you marry
    me?
MARY: Are you quite sure that's what you mean?
SUZUKI: I am student, sorry, a student of English. In the end I
    will be the Professor.
MARY: 'A' Professor is probably what you mean.
SUZUKI: English wife, sorry, a Scottish wife will be very good
    for me.
MARY: You're a good deal younger than I am.
SUZUKI: Five, six years.
    (*Silence.* MARY *looks at him. Eventually she speaks gently.*)
MARY: No, I can't. And now we'd better do a question in
    Japanese.
    (SUZUKI's *pen flies over the paper as he writes something in
    Japanese. When* SUZUKI *finishes he speaks the words.*)
SUZUKI: Will you marry me?
    (MARY *shakes her head. Then she answers in Japanese.*)
MARY: I'm afraid I'm married already.
    (SUZUKI's *jaw drops.*)
    Now, how was that for grammar? And word order?
    (SUZUKI *clears his throat and looks serious.*)
SUZUKI: Quite accurate. Just the pronunciation as usual. Try
    again. I'm afraid I'm married already.
MARY: I'm afraid I'm married already.

SUZUKI: Better.

(He looks down, momentarily a little upset. MARY *consults her watch and reverts to speaking English.)*

MARY: Well, Mr Suzuki, I think our time is up for today.

*(*SUZUKI *nods, begins to gather his notebooks etc., reaches for his briefcase and surprises* MARY *by producing from it something wrapped in a* furoshiki, *which he hands to her.)*

SUZUKI: I have a small present for you.

(He holds out the parcel which, for the moment, MARY *does not accept.)*

MARY: I don't think that's at all necessary, Mr Suzuki.

SUZUKI: Please, I would like you to have it. You do not let me pay. So please allow small present.

MARY: Well, it's very kind of you.

(She takes it from him. He bows to her.)

SUZUKI: Goodnight, Mackenzie San.

MARY: Goodnight, Mr Suzuki. Until next Tuesday.

SUZUKI: Yes. Indeed.

*(*SUZUKI *leaves the room and can be heard leaving the house. After a while,* MARY, *a little puzzled, unwraps the* furoshiki. *It contains a book – evidently, from its size and cover, an art book.* MARY *considers it a moment, rather pleased. Then she opens it.*

MARY's *face: she's astonished. She turns a page, frowning in amazement. From a partial glimpse of the book, it's clear that it's a collection of highly explicit nineteenth-century Japanese pornographic prints.*

MARY's *reactions are various, as she looks up from the book: shock and alarm, tempered by a genuine amusement.*

Eventually she shakes her head, looks down and turns another page.)

EXT. PARK NEAR MARY'S HOUSE. DAY

Summer's day. MARY *and* AIKO *walk in a small local park. Everyone seems to be out with their children, and* MARY *scans the babies among them with conspicuous eagerness. Finally, she stops by a bench and stares at a woman who sits with a baby on her knee.*

AIKO *takes* MARY's *arm.*

AIKO: Don't. You mustn't.

MARY: It's his birthday today.

(AIKO *leads her away as large tears begin to roll down her cheeks.*)

INT. V I P ROOM AT TSUSHIMAYA. DAY
The room is rather heavily furnished in Western style: gilding and tapestries and dark, ornate tables.
When MARY *arrives,* HINOBE *is on his feet, dancing attendance on a woman whose face is not visible at first, and who sits perched on the very edge of her chair, her back ramrod-straight.*
At first, HINOBE *takes no notice of* MARY's *arrival, occupied as he is with offering* yokan *to the woman, which she declines.*
Eventually, he looks up at MARY, *his eyes sparkling with malice.*
HINOBE: Mackenzie San.

(*The woman turns to look at* MARY: *she's the* COUNTESS KURIHAMA *and, as she rises to her feet and bows to* MARY, HINOBE *introduces her in Japanese.*)
This is one of our most important clients: the Countess Kurihama.

(MARY *tries to cover her shock by means of a deep bow: she rises to find the* COUNTESS *staring at her shrewdly, as* HINOBE *looks on.*)

INT. LIVING-ROOM IN MARY'S HOUSE IN TSUKIJI. EVENING
As before: MARY *watches* KENTARO *eating.*
MARY: How does your wife feel about this arrangement?

(KENTARO *looks up at her, surprised.*)

INT. V I P ROOM. DAY
The COUNTESS *considers* MARY *for a moment, before speaking.*
COUNTESS: Miss Mackenzie.
MARY: Yes.

(MARY *has automatically answered in English but the* COUNTESS *now continues in Japanese.*)
COUNTESS: My husband has just been appointed Military Attaché to our Embassy in London.

(*She pauses for a moment, as if waiting for an answer, but* MARY *simply inclines her head.*)
We're due to leave in the New Year; and what I require is a

complete wardrobe for use in England, both formal and
informal wear, everything I may need.

(*She pauses again, and this time* MARY *manages to speak.*)

MARY: Of course. Of course.

INT. NOODLE SHOP. EVENING

MARY *sits hunched in a corner, miserable.* AIKO *faces her, thinking
aloud. Dialogue in English.*

AIKO: I'm sure he doesn't know anything about this. He's only
just back from Korea.

MARY: What can I do?

AIKO: Whatever has to be done. Don't let any of them see how
you feel about this.

MARY: You think she's trying to punish me?

AIKO: Perhaps. But she's probably also heard you make the best
European clothes in Tokyo.

(*She smiles sympathetically at* MARY.)

INT. TSUSHIMA. DAY

HINOBE *approaches* MARY, *his expression exultant. Dialogue in
Japanese.*

HINOBE: The Countess Kurihama will be here at ten.

MARY: I've asked Minagawa San to take her measurements.

HINOBE: No.

MARY: No?

HINOBE: No. With a customer of this importance, you do it
yourself.

(MARY *doesn't answer; she looks at him angrily.*)

INT. CHANGING-ROOM. DAY

MARY *with her tape measure,* MINAGAWA *with a notepad and the*
COUNTESS KURIHAMA *in a thin under-kimono. The atmosphere is
ecclesiastical as* MARY *takes the measurements and murmurs the
relevant numbers for* MINAGAWA *to write down. The* COUNTESS
*stands, following instructions to raise an arm or move a leg, passive,
but radiating a kind of complacent satisfaction.*

*The scene is long enough for various complicated messages to pass
between* MARY *and the* COUNTESS's *mirror-image. Finally,* MARY
on her knees, measuring the outside of the COUNTESS's *leg, is
sufficiently defeated by the situation to close her eyes for a second.*

INT. MARY'S ROOM IN THE MANDARIN'S PALACE IN
MUKDEN. DAY
The old Chinese seamstress, on her knees, making adjustments to
MARY'*s wedding dress.*

INT. CHANGING-ROOM. DAY
MARY *opens her eyes to see the shadow of a smile playing about the*
reflection of the COUNTESS'*s lips. She looks at the tape, says a*
figure. MINAGAWA *writes on her pad.*

INT. FITTING-ROOM. DAY
MINAGAWA *is adjusting one of the wire shapes as* MARY *looks on,*
her mind elsewhere. Suddenly a thought strikes her and she speaks in
Japanese.
MARY: Minagawa San.
MINAGAWA: Yes.
MARY: Is there a list somewhere of the account customers?
MINAGAWA: Of course. In the accounts department.
MARY: With addresses?
MINAGAWA: Well, naturally.
    (MARY *shakes her head and speaks more or less to herself, in*
    English.)
MARY: Why didn't I ever think of that before?

EXT. GARDEN OF KURIHAMA'S HOUSE. NIGHT
MARY *stands in the large garden of a traditional Japanese house,*
constructed from dark wood, on one storey, with the exception of one
upstairs room. It's a midsummer evening and the screens are slid
back, so that most of the ground floor is open to the air. Domestic
sounds and desultory conversations can be heard.
MARY *waits. From where she's standing she can see that* KENTARO
and the COUNTESS *are with a maid, who is clearing the table and*
talking to them. The COUNTESS *answers, and then the two women*
leave the room together.
KENTARO *stands at the window for a moment, then steps down into*
the garden. MARY *moves, so that the light from the house reveals*
her.
KENTARO *masters his shock almost immediately. He hurries over to*
her and takes her arm without a word, leading her firmly away from

83

the house to the furthest recesses of the garden. Only then does he
speak, in a fierce whisper.

KENTARO: How did you find me?

MARY: Does it matter?

KENTARO: I would like to know.

MARY: Where is he?

> (*Silence.* KENTARO *looks away for a moment, controlling*
> *himself with difficulty.*)

KENTARO: He is with good people. I promise you.

MARY: Where?

KENTARO: I chose very carefully.

> (MARY *also makes a great effort to overcome her rage and*
> *emotion.*)

MARY: I heard you were going to England.

KENTARO: Yes.

MARY: Well, don't you think he should have at least one parent
in this country who knows where he is?

KENTARO: The people he is with. They are his parents.

MARY: I could walk into that house and make a very ugly scene.

> (KENTARO *sighs; then he speaks quietly, with some dignity.*)

KENTARO: I'm going in now. You must do what you think is
best.

> (*He turns and walks away from her. She takes a step after*
> *him, then stops. She watches him disappear into the house. For*
> *a moment she stands, racked with indecision. Then finally she*
> *turns and hurries away into the night.*)

INT. HINOBE'S OFFICE. DAY

HINOBE's *office is a miniature version of* TSUSHIMA's.

MARY *enters the room.*

HINOBE, *behind his desk, takes absolutely no notice of her. She*
waits for a while, then speaks, in Japanese.

MARY: You asked to see me?

> (HINOBE *looks up at her, his expression venomous.*)

HINOBE: I understand, this morning, you were not present at
the Countess Kurihama's fitting.

MARY: I have a cold. I thought it better that Minagawa San . . .

HINOBE: You thought? You thought? Did I not give you exact
instructions in this matter.

MARY: You did. But I decided . . .

(HINOBE *interrupts* MARY, *crashing his fist down on his desk.*)

HINOBE: You mean to say you deliberately ignored my orders?

MARY: No. It was simply . . .

HINOBE: Don't interrupt! How dare you behave in this way? This will be reported, I can assure you of that! And if I have anything to do with it, you'll finish up back where you belong! On the streets!

(*By the time he reaches the climax of his speech, he's yelling his head off at her. She waits, impassive. As he finishes, however, both of them are startled by the sudden arrival of* TSUSHIMA. HINOBE *leaps to his feet and bows, and then opens his mouth to speak, but* TSUSHIMA's *quiet voice cuts in, speaking to* MARY.)

TSUSHIMA: Would you be so good as to excuse us, Mackenzie San?

(MARY *acknowledges this with a slight bow, then hurries from the room.*)

INT. TSUSHIMAYA. DAY

MARY *stands at her station, her attention elsewhere, so that she's startled by the sudden arrival of* MINAGAWA SAN.

MINAGAWA: Tsushima San wants to see you in his office.

MARY: When?

MINAGAWA: Right now.

INT. HIROSHI TSUSHIMA'S OFFICE. DAY

MARY, *seated, sips at her tea.* TSUSHIMA *is comfortably in the middle of one of his disconcerting silences.*

MARY *waits.*

Eventually, TSUSHIMA *looks up at her.*

TSUSHIMA: 180 yen a month.

MARY: I'm sorry?

TSUSHIMA: Your starting salary as head of department.

MARY: But Hinobe . . .

TSUSHIMA: Mr Hinobe needs a change, I feel. He has perhaps been stuck in one place for too long. We had a vacancy and I have asked him to take over the toy department.

MARY: I see.

TSUSHIMA: In Nagoya.

(*Silence.* TSUSHIMA *contemplates* MARY *for a moment.*)

We have never had a female head of department.

MARY: I'm honoured.

TSUSHIMA: This may not be a popular decision. But we have always been a progressive company. And I'm sure you will be able to cope with the extra work your position will entail.

MARY: I hope so.

TSUSHIMA: I know so. And in preparation for all your hard work, I think it only fair that you should have a holiday.

MARY: Thank you.

TSUSHIMA: So take . . . (*He breaks off to consider.*)

MARY: Yes?

TSUSHIMA: Take two days.

EXT. VERANDA OF BARON ONNODERA'S HOUSE IN KAMAKURA. DAY

MARY *and* AIKO *are on the veranda overlooking an exquisite walled garden. The house,* AIKO'*s ex-husband's summer villa in the resort of Kamakura, is an unusually large two-storey building of traditional Japanese design.*

The sun beats down on the ornamental fishpond.

MARY *looks more relaxed than at any time since her arrival in Japan.*

Dialogue in English.

MARY: Your husband . . .

AIKO: My ex-husband.

MARY: Your ex-husband. He doesn't mind you using his villa?

AIKO: Why should he?

MARY: If my ex-husband had a villa . . .

AIKO: But he was a barbarian.

MARY: Yes. Or an Englishman, as we say in Scotland.

(*She smiles and turns, heading back into the house.*)

INT. SITTING-ROOM IN THE HOUSE. DAY

AIKO *follows* MARY *into an exquisite sitting-room, furnished in the Japanese style, with painted wall-panels.*

MARY: I hope you're proud of me. The first woman head of department at Tsushimaya.

AIKO: Yes. I'm not so sure I approve it should be a foreigner.

MARY: You don't like foreigners either.

AIKO: I think you understand the point I'm making.
MARY: Yes. Yes, I do.

EXT. BARON ONNODERA'S HOUSE. NIGHT
*Moonlight on the walled garden. The nearby pagoda is sharply
etched against a silver sky.*

INT. DINING-ROOM IN THE HOUSE. NIGHT
*The dining-room, surprisingly, is furnished in European style: a
dresser full of plates, a polished table and an elaborate chandelier,
disproportionate to the height of the room.* MARY *is wearing an
elegant dark kimono. Two maids serve a meal, the food set out like
beautiful flower arrangements.*
AIKO: He brought this stuff back with him from Europe. I told
    him to give it to charity. It looks absurd here.
    (*The maids leave the room as* AIKO *becomes aware that*
    MARY's *thoughts are elsewhere.*)
AIKO: What's the matter?
MARY: Taro. Do you suppose they gave him to rich people?
AIKO: I doubt it. He would have looked for modest parents in
    settled circumstances. Not rich people.
MARY: Do you know who they are?
    (AIKO *looks at* MARY *and shakes her head gently.*)
AIKO: No. No idea. I promise you.
    (MARY *broods, lost in thought.*)

INT. TSUSHIMAYA. DAY
It's 8.15, and now it's MARY *who is addressing the serried ranks of
her department. She's prepared her speech in Japanese very carefully
and has now reached its final sentences. The* EMPLOYEES *are all
watching her intently.*
MARY: I want you to feel able to come and talk to me about any
    problems you may have. And finally I'd like to say that if
    you will all be tolerant with me, I think I can promise to be
    tolerant with you.
    (*She pauses. Her speech appears to have gone down quite well.*)
    And now may we practise our greeting?
    (*The* EMPLOYEES *reply as one, chanting their formula.*)
EMPLOYEES: Welcome to Tsushimaya. Is there any way in
    which I might be of assistance to you?

87

(MARY *beams at them.*)
MARY: Very good. Carry on.

INT. TSUSHIMAYA STORE. DAY
Montage: MARY *oversees her department, visits the sewing-room, works in her office on new designs, talks to a customer, finally arrives at* TSUSHIMA's *office.*

INT. HIROSHI TSUSHIMA'S OFFICE. DAY
TSUSHIMA *looks up as* MARY *enters the room, then he looks down again.*
MARY *waits.*
Eventually, she speaks, in Japanese.
MARY: You asked to see me?
    (*It's some time before* TSUSHIMA *looks up again.*)
TSUSHIMA: The Countess Kurihama has cancelled her order.
    Everything. She wants none of it.
MARY: I see.
TSUSHIMA: Can you think of a reason?
    (*Silence.*
    Then MARY *decides in favour of boldness. She speaks this one sentence in English.*)
MARY: I think you are probably aware of the circumstances, Mr
    Tsushima.
    (TSUSHIMA *considers her shrewdly for a while.*)
TSUSHIMA: As long as it's that, and not bad workmanship.
MARY: I think I can assure you . . .
TSUSHIMA: In that case, we shall sustain the loss. You may go.
MARY: Thank you.

INT. SITTING-ROOM IN ALICIA BASSETT-HILL'S HOUSE.
EVENING. 1907
MARY *has* EMMA LOU's *new baby,* RICHARD, *on her knee.* EMMA
LOU *sits watching them, gnawing at her lip.*
ALICIA *is crossing the room with a teapot.*
ALICIA: I'll just freshen the pot.
    (*She leaves the room and* EMMA LOU *glances at her watch.*)
EMMA LOU: Bob has gotten more Japanese than the Japanese,
    the hours he works, I mean. But I guess I'd better get
    back, case he's on time for once.

MARY: Don't go.
> (*She strokes the top of the baby's head, a strange expression on her face.*)

EMMA LOU: Boy, the kids really like you. And you like them too, am I right?

MARY: Yes, I do.
> (EMMA LOU *hesitates. She looks nervous.*)

EMMA LOU: Can we have lunch one day?

MARY: I work most days, but of course.

EMMA LOU: What it is, I . . . I need a friend. I'm real scared.

MARY: Why?

EMMA LOU: I think I may be pregnant again.

MARY: I see.

EMMA LOU: And I don't even know if I'm cut out to be a mother. It doesn't come, well, you know, it doesn't feel so natural. Bob doesn't understand, he just wants a lot of kids, and I just feel . . . I feel so lonely.

MARY: I think I understand.

EMMA LOU: I can't seem to function in this country, you know what I mean?
> (MARY *doesn't answer for a moment; she contemplates the baby painfully as he plays with her buttons.* EMMA LOU *seems about to speak again, but thinks better of it as* ALICIA *breezes back into the room with a steaming teapot.*)

INT. LIVING-ROOM IN MARY'S HOUSE. NIGHT
MARY is reading, and looks up sharply; she's heard some sort of sound in the garden. She puts down her book and moves as quietly as she can out into:

INT. HALLWAY. NIGHT
The tiny hallway, at present in darkness. There's an umbrella stand there, containing a stout bamboo and oil-paper umbrella, which MARY eases gingerly out of the stand. Then she rests it against the wall and, simultaneously, slides back the front door and switches the light on.

EXT. MARY'S HOUSE. NIGHT
A shaft of light falls into the yard, illuminating a pair of feet, whose owner immediately attempts to shuffle them back into the shadow.

Too late, however, for MARY, *who has seized her umbrella, raced into the yard and dealt the intruder a stinging blow.*

AKIRA SUZUKI *steps into the light, groaning and rubbing the side of his head.*

MARY, *startled, exclaims in English.*

MARY: Mr Suzuki!

SUZUKI: Yes. A very good evening to you.

MARY: Come inside.

SUZUKI: No, really . . .

MARY: Come on!

> (MARY *drags* SUZUKI, *protesting feebly and rubbing at his head, into the house, in the doorway of which* MARY's *maid,* HANAKO, *has now appeared, her eyes wide with amazement.*)

INT. LIVING-ROOM IN MARY'S HOUSE. NIGHT

SUZUKI *sips at some tea, his expression a mixture of shame and righteous indignation.*

MARY *speaks to him in English.*

MARY: So the meeting in the tram, all that . . .

SUZUKI: Yes.

MARY: Everything was arranged by Count Kurihama?

SUZUKI: He asked me to inform him how you were.

MARY: What about the proposal? And . . . the rest?

> (SUZUKI *looks down and finally mumbles an answer.*)

SUZUKI: That was my idea.

> (MARY *smiles.*)

MARY: I see. Suppose it had worked? The Count wouldn't have been very happy.

SUZUKI: Yes, but I would.

MARY: (*Shakes her head, still smiling*) And now?

SUZUKI: He leaves for England next week. He wanted a final report.

MARY: I see.

SUZUKI: I think I must go now.

MARY: Suzuki.

SUZUKI: Yes.

MARY: Do you know where my son is?

SUZUKI: No.

MARY: Why don't you tell me?

SUZUKI: I don't know.

MARY: If the Count's going to England, he won't know, I just
       want . . . I won't make a nuisance of myself, I just need to
       know where he is!
       (SUZUKI *scrambles to his feet.*)
SUZUKI: I swear. On my honour. I have no idea.
       (MARY *is trying not to burst into tears.*
       SUZUKI *bows and hurries from the room.*)

INT. MARY'S BEDROOM. NIGHT
It's late, but MARY's *light is still on. She lies between her quilts,
remembering.*

EXT. PRECINCTS OF THE ASAKUSA TEMPLE. NIGHT
At the Festival of the Dead: TARO *reaches forward to tug at*
MARY's *hair.*

INT. MARY'S BEDROOM. NIGHT
MARY *lies in silence, tears rolling down her cheeks.*

INT. HIROSHI TSUSHIMA'S OFFICE. DAY. 1909
MARY *sits opposite* TSUSHIMA, *supplied this time with tea and rice
biscuits. He seems slightly more affable than usual.*
Dialogue in Japanese, at which MARY *is now noticeably more
proficient.*
TSUSHIMA: How long have you been with us now?
MARY: Just over three years.
TSUSHIMA: It's been a most happy and successful association, at
       least from our point of view.
MARY: I've been very grateful for the opportunities you've given
       me.
TSUSHIMA: And all your initiatives have had very profitable
       results: the shows . . . the links you've established with
       Lancashire and Paris, the English Christmas, all excellent.
MARY: Thank you.
       (TSUSHIMA *pauses, looking penetratingly across at* MARY.)
TSUSHIMA: That's why I feel sure you're the right person for a
       very important task I have in mind.
MARY: Oh?
       (TSUSHIMA *pauses again for effect, studying his fingernails.*)

91

TSUSHIMA: I want you to go and effect the same transformation in the ladies' clothing department in our store in Nagoya.
(*Silence.* MARY *frowns, thinking hard.*)
MARY: I'm not sure I want to leave Tokyo.
(TSUSHIMA *looks up at her sharply.*)
TSUSHIMA: It would only be for two or three years.
MARY: That seems a very long time to leave the life I've made for myself here.
TSUSHIMA: In Japan, an employee generally follows the instructions of his or her company without question.
MARY: Does Mr Hinobe still work in Nagoya?
TSUSHIMA: Certainly. Figures in the toy department have been most encouraging.
(*He glowers at her for a moment across the desk.*)
Perhaps you need a holiday to consider this proposal.
MARY: Two days?
TSUSHIMA: Take four.
(*He looks at her shrewdly.*)
Take a week.
MARY: Thank you.
TSUSHIMA: I do want you to have time enough to be able to arrive at the correct decision.

EXT. BARON ONNODERA'S HOUSE IN KAMAKURA. DAY
The house. Hot summer's day.

INT. DINING-ROOM IN THE HOUSE. DAY
MARY, BOB *and* EMMA LOU DALE *are guests in the Baron's house.*
BOB JR, CHARLES *and* RICHARD *are now six, four and three and the new baby,* DANIEL, *nestles in* MARY's *arms.*
EMMA LOU *is once again pregnant, though this time not yet visibly so.*
EMMA LOU: Well, I don't think you should let them order you around.
MARY: I'm afraid in this country employees do exactly what they're told; and it is a very good job.
EMMA LOU: But I don't know what we would do if you left Tokyo.
BOB: I guess we have to let Mary make her own decisions, dear.
EMMA LOU: It isn't her decision, that's what I'm saying.

BOB: It's her decision if she wants to agree to their decision.
EMMA LOU: You just think women should do what they're told and ask no questions.
BOB: I don't think anything of the kind.
EMMA LOU: Oh, you don't, uh?
  (*Her tone is far from friendly:* MARY *tries to rescue the situation.*)
MARY: Why don't you two take yourselves down to the beach. I'll give the children their lunch.
  (*Neither of them answers: they're glaring at each other, their expressions openly hostile.*)

EXT. VERANDA. DAY
MARY *settles* DANIEL *into his pram in a shaded part of the veranda.*

INT. DINING-ROOM. DAY
MARY *is having lunch with the children. She is cutting up* RICHARD's *food for him.*

EXT. HOUSE. DAY
Everything seems normal. The pram is on the veranda. All of a sudden, the birds stop singing, and an oppressive silence falls.

INT. DINING-ROOM. DAY
The chandelier: its glass drops begin, ever so gently, to vibrate and tinkle. MARY *looks up, frowning. Very gradually, the crockery on the table begins to rattle and dance.* MARY's *initial reaction is slow: for a moment, it is as if she is paralysed. Quite suddenly, there is a great roaring rumble, and the chandelier begins to yaw violently. Plates begin to fall off the dresser and smash.*
MARY *leaps to her feet and rushes out of the room.*

INT. SITTING-ROOM. DAY
MARY *races across the room.*

EXT. VERANDA. DAY
MARY *appears, scoops* DANIEL *out of his pram and turns back into the house.*

93

INT. DINING-ROOM. DAY
The chandelier is now swinging so violently, it is hitting the ceiling. MARY *arrives back,* DANIEL *in her arms, to the relief of the terrified children. As she appears, the rumbling stops and an abrupt silence falls, interrupted only by the jangle of glass in the chandelier. One of the children whimpers.*
MARY: It's all right. It's all right now.
    (RICHARD *runs over to her and buries his face in her skirt. She smiles, gasping with relief.*)
It's all right.
(*The words are scarcely out of her mouth, when the roaring suddenly starts again, this time far more thunderous than the initial tremor. Once again, the chandelier smashes full tilt into the ceiling.* MARY's *voice is calm, but extremely firm.*)
Under the table.
(*The boys all scramble under the table.* MARY *hands the baby in to* BOB *and then climbs in with them. They huddle under the table.*
As the earthquake reaches its apogee, the chandelier breaks loose and shatters on the polished surface of the table.)

EXT. HOUSE. DAY
As before the earthquake, an eerie calm and silence have ensued. Smoke drifts across the garden.

INT. DINING-ROOM. EVENING
Candles are lit and EMMA LOU *sits at the table, sobbing hysterically, surrounded by glittering fragments of debris.* BOB *stands awkwardly in the vicinity, and* MARY, *now in a kimono, holds* EMMA LOU's *hand.*
EMMA LOU: We got to get back to Tokyo right now, you hear?
BOB: There isn't going to be another one.
EMMA LOU: You get me out of here!
BOB: We have two more days of our holiday.
EMMA LOU: You can stay, if you like. We're getting out.
    (BOB *looks at* MARY *for guidance. She is stroking* EMMA LOU's *hand.*)
MARY: I expect it might be best to go back in the morning.

INT. MARY'S BEDROOM IN THE BARON'S HOUSE. NIGHT
MARY *is awake when* EMMA LOU *comes tiptoeing into the room.*
EMMA LOU: Mary?
MARY: I'm awake.
EMMA LOU: Are you all right? I'm sorry I took it so badly.
　　(MARY *beckons her over and she goes to perch on the side of*
　　MARY'*s bed.* MARY *lights a candle, then tries the bedside light*
　　switch, but the electricity is evidently still not working.)
MARY: I don't know why, but it's helped me make a decision.
　　I'm going to refuse to go to Nagoya.
EMMA LOU: Oh, great.
　　(*She takes* MARY'*s hand.*)
　　Listen, I'm pregnant again.
MARY: Are you?
EMMA LOU: I haven't told Bob. I'm so scared he'll stop me
　　going back to see my folks in September.
MARY: Why should he do that? It means you can have this one
　　at home, perhaps.
EMMA LOU: Oh, yes. That would be wonderful.
　　(*She reflects for a moment.*)
　　Not as wonderful as if I didn't have to have it at all.
　　(MARY *cannot help a spasm of pain crossing her face.*)
MARY: Don't say that.
　　(EMMA LOU *does not notice her distress; she is lost in thought*
　　for a moment.)
EMMA LOU: This thing, this thing happening, it's made me
　　think differently as well.

INT. HIROSHI TSUSHIMA'S OFFICE. DAY
TSUSHIMA *is evidently far from pleased. He sits glowering across at*
MARY. *Eventually, he speaks. Dialogue in Japanese.*
TSUSHIMA: It's really a matter of principle. I can't begin
　　allowing people to refuse postings.
MARY: I understand.
TSUSHIMA: Besides, they're already expecting you in Nagoya.
MARY: I'm very sorry.
　　(TSUSHIMA *rearranges one or two small objects on his desk.*)
TSUSHIMA: It's not a question of salary?
MARY: Not at all, no.
TSUSHIMA: Well, this is most regrettable.

95

(MARY *startles him considerably by rising to her feet.*)
The interview is not yet finished.
MARY: All the same, I think you'll find there's nothing more to
be said.
(*She bows deeply and hurries out of the room, leaving*
TSUSHIMA *entirely bemused.*)

EXT. THE KANSAS AND MIDWEST WARRANTY TRUST BANK.
DAY
The office is so identified by a bilingual brass plaque. MARY *checks
she is at the right place and then strides decisively in.*

INT. BOB DALE'S OFFICE. DAY
BOB *gets up as* MARY *enters and shows her to a seat. He seems
uneasy.*
BOB: Well, now, this is a pleasure.
MARY: Thank you for agreeing to see me.
BOB: Is this something about Emma Lou?
MARY: No, it isn't, it isn't. It's about me.
BOB: Oh.
(*He takes a seat behind his desk.*)
MARY: I remember you said it was hard to get the Japanese
interested in accepting a loan. Is it getting any easier?
BOB: Some. But I wouldn't say it was like shooting fish in a
barrel.
MARY: Well, I just wanted to tell you that I'm more than
willing to accept a loan.
(BOB *looks up at her, astonished.*)

INT. NOODLE SHOP. EVENING
MARY *is entertaining* MINAGAWA SAN *to dinner. They're eating
heartily, the atmosphere between them intimate. Dialogue in
Japanese.*
MARY: And how much is he paying you?
MINAGAWA: Fifty a month.
MARY: It's very mean.
MINAGAWA: It's more than I've ever earned.
MARY: You're worth twice that.
(*She looks up at her for a moment and then goes on
impulsively.*)

96

If I offered you a job that did pay twice that, what would
you say?

(MINAGAWA SAN *looks up at her.*)

MINAGAWA: I'd come and work for you whatever you offered
me. (*She smiles.*) Although twice the money would be very
acceptable. Yes.

(*She's said the last word in English.*

MARY *smiles back at her.*)

INT. BOB DALE'S OFFICE. DAY

MARY *has a draft contract spread out on* BOB's *desk. She's coming
to the end of studying it.*

BOB: Not bad, uh?

(MARY *looks up at him.*)

MARY: Not very good, either.

BOB: What do you mean?

MARY: I need more capital, I want premises on a worthwhile
site, preferably in the Ginza. I have to equip them, and I
want to employ half-a-dozen girls in the workroom as well
as the shop staff.

BOB: Well, we're open to discussion on that.

MARY: If the Bank has a sixty per cent holding, it means you
can get rid of me if you want to, doesn't it?

BOB: I guess, in theory.

MARY: And you ask for forty per cent of the profits.

BOB: That's normal.

MARY: That's not going to make it very easy for me to expand
the business, is it?

BOB: You have a better suggestion?

MARY: I don't know if it's better. It's very simple. I want
30,000 yen capital.

BOB: Wait a minute.

MARY: You can have a forty per cent holding and twenty per
cent of the profits. I think those are the main points.

BOB: It's out of the question.

MARY: Otherwise I shall just have to go back to teaching
English to Japanese students.

BOB: I didn't know you did that.

MARY: Oh, yes. One of my pupils was so pleased with his
results he wanted to marry me.

97

(Silence. BOB doesn't quite know if he's being made fun of. He considers this, frowning.)

BOB: You'd better let me think about this.

MARY: Don't think too long.

BOB: What do you mean?

MARY: I only mean my savings are running low.

INT. CABIN ON THE SS EMPRESS OF RUSSIA. DAY

MARY, BOB, EMMA LOU, *now noticeably more pregnant, and the four children are crowded into* EMMA LOU's *single cabin.*

EMMA LOU: Bob.

BOB: What is it?

EMMA LOU: Take the kids to their cabin. I want to say goodbye to Mary.

BOB: OK. Come on, Bob.

(He shepherds the children out. When he's gone, EMMA LOU waits for a moment and then embraces MARY. She's close to tears. She speaks very quietly.)

EMMA LOU: I'm not coming back.

MARY: What?

EMMA LOU: You're fine here, you know how to handle it. I never understood a single thing about it.

MARY: Does Bob know?

EMMA LOU: I didn't tell him.

MARY: Why are you doing it?

EMMA LOU: After this one, I just can't have any more children. It's eating me alive. Do you understand that?

(MARY is suddenly very moved. She hangs on to EMMA LOU tightly.

BOB reappears in the cabin. He frowns, a little surprised at the intensity of the scene.)*

EXT. ENTRANCE TO MARY'S HOUSE. NIGHT

MARY *opens the door cautiously and is puzzled to find* BOB DALE. *A certain aggressiveness in his demeanour is the only sign he has been drinking.*

MARY: Bob?

BOB: May I come in?

INT. LIVING-ROOM IN MARY'S HOUSE. NIGHT
BOB *steps into the room and draws a document out of his inside pocket with a flourish.*
BOB: Your contract.
MARY: Oh?
BOB: Emma Lou made me promise to give it to you.
   (*He hands it to her.*)
MARY: Thank you.
BOB: We ought to celebrate. You got a drink? I need a drink. I need a lot of drinks.
MARY: Haven't you had several already?
BOB: Yes, well. I just figured something out. She isn't coming back, is she?
   (MARY *doesn't answer.*)
BOB: How's about if I spent the night?
   (MARY *contemplates him calmly.*)
MARY: Go home, Bob.
BOB: Home? What home?
   (*He's answered explosively: now his eyes fill with tears.*)
   I'm sorry.
   (*She indicates the contract.*)
MARY: Thank you for this.
BOB: Yeah.
   (*He turns and stumbles out of the room.*)

EXT. TSUSHIMAYA. DAY
MARY *stops* MINAGAWA SAN, *as she leaves the store after her day's work.* MARY *waves the contract, excitedly, speaking in Japanese.*
MARY: I've got the money. Can you start next month?
   (MINAGAWA SAN *smiles and nods.*)

INT. LIVING-ROOM IN MARY'S HOUSE. DAY
The patterns are out again, spread all over the floor. MARY *is working on them. There's a knock at the door.*

INT. HALLWAY/YARD. DAY
MARY *slides back the door. It's* KENTARO KURIHAMA. *They stand for a moment, looking at each other in silence.*
MARY: Where's my son?
KENTARO: Should I go away?

(*Long silence.* MARY *looks at him, swept by contradictory emotions.*)

MARY: No. Come in.

INT. LIVING-ROOM. DAY

KENTARO, *sitting on the floor, makes a gesture to take in the room.*

KENTARO: This is very . . .

MARY: It's all right.

KENTARO: You could have stayed in the house, it was your house, you could have stayed.

MARY: No, I couldn't.

KENTARO: I hear you've left Tsushimaya.

MARY: We had a disagreement.

KENTARO: What are you going to do?

MARY: Start my own business.

(KENTARO *frowns disapprovingly.*)

KENTARO: What kind of business?

MARY: Clothes. I know a lot about it now.

(KENTARO *considers for a moment.*)

KENTARO: You must allow me to invest.

MARY: No.

(*He shifts uncomfortably.*)

KENTARO: You've changed.

MARY: I had to.

(*Pause. Then* MARY *cuts off what he's about to say.*)

How was England?

KENTARO: This time I was happier. And I think when the war comes in Europe, we will fight on England's side.

MARY: Is there war coming in Europe?

KENTARO: I think so. Everybody wants it.

(MARY *shakes her head dismissively.*)

I was going to say. Have you forgotten me?

(MARY *looks up at him, clear-eyed.*)

MARY: Never.

EXT. YARD. DAY

KENTARO *leaves the house. Then he turns back to speak to* MARY, *who's standing in the doorway.*

KENTARO: Can I see you again?

(*Again, there's a hesitation from* MARY.)

MARY: I don't know. I must think.

KENTARO: I'll write to you.

MARY: Don't have me followed again. I don't want that.

(KENTARO, *somewhat taken aback by this, eventually nods in agreement.*)

KENTARO: I think of you every day.

MARY: And every day I think of him.

(KENTARO *nods again, thoughtful. Then he bows and turns away.*

MARY *keeps a fierce grip on the door-frame as she watches him leave.*)

FOUR

EXT. STREET IN YOKOHAMA. DAY
*It's 1935. A closed Dodge convertible slows to a halt, obliged to do
so by a column of soldiers crossing its path.*

INT. DODGE. YOKOHAMA STREET. DAY
MARY *is the passenger in the Dodge, which is being driven by*
KOMORO, *her uniformed chauffeur. She's fifty-two now. She looks
relatively serene and contented. The years seem to have treated her
well.*
*She looks out at the soldiers, all very young with sternly impassive
expressions, as they proceed at a slow goose-step. Flags hang out of
the window of a nearby apartment block.*
MARY *leans forward and addresses* KOMORO *in Japanese. She's
now completely fluent.*
MARY: Where are they going?
KOMORO: On board ship and then to China.
MARY: Lot of flags.
KOMORO: A flag in the window means a son at the front.
MARY: I see. (*She leans back in her seat.*) I think they look
ridiculous.
   (KOMORO *turns to look back at her, his expression
   unmistakably disapproving.*)
KOMORO: They look magnificent. They could conquer the
world.
   (*He turns back.* MARY *frowns and continues to look out of the
   window.*)

INT. CUSTOMS SHED. DAY
MARY *waits, watching excitedly as* ISABELLE DE
CHAMONPIERRE, *who's now almost sixty, moves to the barrier.
They embrace.*
MARY: It's wonderful to see you.
ISABELLE: I can scarcely believe I'm here.
MARY: I was so sorry to hear about Armand.
ISABELLE: Yes, I miss him very much.

103

EXT. MARY'S HOUSE ON THE BLUFF IN YOKOHAMA. DAY
*The Dodge pulls up outside a two-storey house, green and white,
with balconies on both floors and grey tiles, set in a large garden
overlooking Yokohama Bay. It's an old house. Late nineteenth-
century, built for foreigners and therefore not Japanese in design or
feeling, particularly with regard to the french windows with outside
shutters. A smaller building at the back, virtually windowless and
far more Japanese in character, forms the servants' quarters.*
*MARY and ISABELLE descend from the Dodge, and ISABELLE
stops to look up at the house, clearly full of admiration. She follows
MARY into the front garden and stops half-way up the path to point
at a pretty little tree with red leaves.*
ISABELLE: *C'est joli.*
> (*MARY reaches out, breaks off a leaf and crushes it between her
> fingers.*)
MARY: My gardener wanted to cut it down, he thinks it looks
untidy, but I wouldn't let him. In the big earthquake, in
'23, the house collapsed and it burned away to a black
stump. The following spring it started to grow back. The
gardener distrusts it, he says it must be foreign. A resilient
foreigner. But I like it. (*She holds up her hand for ISABELLE
to sniff the crushed leaf.*) It smells of ginger. Armand would
have known its proper name.

INT. DRAWING-ROOM. MARY'S HOUSE. DAY
*MARY's maid, TOBA, is on her way out of the room. MARY sits,
looking across at ISABELLE, who's sipping her coffee.*
ISABELLE: Armand was much happier after he resigned his
commission. He liked much better the university, he felt at
home there.
MARY: He was a botanist, not a soldier.
ISABELLE: Yes. Only I was a little regretful. I always had a
weakness for uniforms.
MARY: Well, you've come to the right country.

EXT. IMPERIAL HOTEL. DAY
*The Dodge pulls up outside Frank Lloyd Wright's startling
Mexican-style building and MARY and ISABELLE emerge when
KOMORO opens their door. MARY speaks to KOMORO in Japanese.*
MARY: Pick us up in an hour, will you?

(KOMORO *bows in acknowledgement as* MARY *shepherds*
ISABELLE *into the hotel.*)

INT. HOTEL LOBBY. DAY
MARY *and* ISABELLE *cross the crowded lobby, heading for* MARY's
*shop, which is on a prime site in the arcade. Her name is on the shop
in* Romanji *as well as in* Japanese *and the window is full of
fashionable and obviously expensive Western clothes.*
ISABELLE *follows* MARY *into the shop.*

INT. MARY'S SHOP. DAY
*A rather stout middle-aged lady looks up from behind the counter:
this is* MINAGAWA SAN. MARY *points her out to* ISABELLE.
MARY: This is my manageress, Minagawa San, she's been my
    right hand now for twenty-five years.
    (*She speaks to* MINAGAWA *in* Japanese.)
    This is my visitor from France, Isabelle de Chamonpierre.
    (MINAGAWA SAN *bows to* ISABELLE, *then shakes hands with
    her, smiling shyly.*)
MINAGAWA SAN: *Bonjour, Madame.*
MARY: I'm going to take her into the office for a while, perhaps
    you'll join us.
MINAGAWA SAN: In a while, if I can.
    (*And with this,* MARY *leads* ISABELLE *through to her office.*)

INT. PRIVATE OFFICE IN MARY'S SHOP. DAY
MARY *goes and sits behind her desk, indicating the most comfortable
chair to* ISABELLE.
MARY: This shop probably saved my life. The hotel was
    designed by Frank Lloyd Wright and after the earthquake
    it was one of the only buildings in this area left standing.
    My shops in the Ginza and in Yokohama were piles of
    rubble; like my house.
    (ISABELLE *looks thoughtfully around this opulent little room.*)

EXT. KARUIZAWA. EVENING
*The Dodge drives through the pine forest on the outskirts of
Karuizawa. It bumps up a drive and comes to a halt in front of a
chalet in the dying light.*

INT. CHALET. NIGHT
There's a wood-fire in the grate. MARY *and* ISABELLE *sit, nursing china tumblers of warm sake.*

ISABELLE: I always wanted to visit Japan and of course I
    wanted to see you again after all these years; but I also had
    a, what is it called, an ulterior motive.

MARY: What's that?

ISABELLE: I want to persuade you to come back to Europe.

MARY: Why?

ISABELLE: I read the newspapers. First our old Manchuria,
    what do they call it now?

MARY: Manchukuo.

ISABELLE: And then the bombing of Shanghai. These are
    dangerous times here.

MARY: I read the newspapers too; things don't seem very much
    better in Europe.

ISABELLE: It's different.
    (*Silence.* MARY *considers for a moment.*)

MARY: I could sell up everything here and live very comfortably
    in London for the rest of my life. Or even in Edinburgh, I
    suppose. But you know something? Those places seem even
    more fantastic to me now than I imagined Manchuria
    would be, when I went in over the border in a cattle truck.

ISABELLE: Travel is easier these days.

MARY: Maybe I'll visit one day. But it's not only my work
    which keeps me here. There are other things. More
    important things.

ISABELLE: As soon as I saw your house in Yokohama, I knew I
    would never succeed to lure you away.

MARY: I love my house. But it isn't that either.
    (*She reaches over to pour another drink for* ISABELLE.)

EXT. CHALET. DAY
The low early-morning sun slants through the pine trees. MARY *emerges from the chalet to greet* ISABELLE, *who's back from an exploratory walk.*

ISABELLE: It's so beautiful here.
    (MARY *nods in agreement, looking around her.*)

MARY: I first came up here about twenty years ago. Looking for
    my son. I hired a private detective, he was on my payroll

for months. Eventually he assured me he'd traced my boy. He said he was living with a family in the town. But it was a false alarm.

EXT. PINE FOREST. DAY
MARY *and* ISABELLE *stroll through the pine forest.* ISABELLE *shakes her head compassionately.*
ISABELLE: So you never found him?
MARY: Not even the remotest lead. He'll be nearly thirty now. What worries me most is he's almost certain to have gone into the army. I keep on imagining him on some battlefield in Manchuria.
ISABELLE: I see now.
MARY: What?
ISABELLE: That's why you want to stay in Japan.
MARY: No, I've given up hope of ever finding him.
(*They walk on for a moment in silence.*)
ISABELLE: Then is it your friends out here?
MARY: I haven't made that many friends.

INT. WORKROOM. DAY
MARY *moves with* MINAGAWA SAN *through the large, airy workroom she's supplied for her dress-making staff. The girls greet her respectfully but without constraint.*
MARY: (*Voice over*) There's Minagawa San, of course, and the people who work for me.

INT. DINING-ROOM IN AIKO'S HOUSE. EVENING
In the small dining-room of AIKO's *very modest house,* MARY *is being harangued by* KATSUGI, *a small, overweight, balding man of about forty. We can't hear what he's saying, but his expression is hectoring and his gestures emphatic.*
AIKO *comes into the room with a carafe of sake and drops to her knees beside him to serve him; he holds out his cup without looking at her.* AIKO *exchanges a glance with* MARY.
MARY: (*Voice over*) And my friend Aiko married a much younger man, Katsugi, a member of the Socialist Party, who's always explaining to me what a wicked exploiter I am, while treating her like dirt. You know women still don't have the vote in this country, and if Aiko's husband

is an example of a progressive, I don't see how they ever will.

EXT. PINE WOODS. DAY

MARY *and* ISABELLE *have reached a spot where a clearing gives a spectacular view of the surrounding mountains. They sit on a bench, looking out at the vista.* ISABELLE *is listening intently.*

MARY: I spoke to her about it once, when he hadn't been home for a week, and she told me she was well aware of all the disadvantages, but that she needed him and she knew life would be worse without him.
(*She looks up at* ISABELLE *for a moment, before continuing.*)
And I suppose that's how I feel.
(ISABELLE *frowns for a moment, then suddenly understands what* MARY *is saying.*)

ISABELLE: You mean you still see him?

MARY: Yes. I do.
(MARY *looks out at the view for a moment, her eyes distant.*)
I do.

ISABELLE: Well, now I understand.

INT. DRAWING-ROOM OF MARY'S HOUSE IN YOKOHAMA. EVENING

ISABELLE *is examining a* shogi *board and its pieces: the board is laid out on* MARY'S *coffee table in the main room of her house, the furnishings of which are a compromise between European and Japanese, the whole effect one of elegant economy.*

MARY: It's the Japanese version of chess; it's called *shogi*. The first time I played it, with Kentaro, I asked him which piece was the Queen. He laughed and said there was no Queen; that war was a game for men.
(ISABELLE *smiles, then she looks admiringly round the room.*)

ISABELLE: You've done so well.

MARY: I suppose I have. But it's no substitute.

INT. HALLWAY OF MARY'S HOUSE. DAY

ISABELLE'S *luggage is being carried out of the house. She's wearing a coat. She and* MARY *embrace.*

ISABELLE: *La prochaine fois à Paris, n'est-ce pas?*

MARY: I hope so.

ISABELLE: Thank you for all your kindness.

MARY: I think you've forgiven me my bad behaviour in Mukden, haven't you?

ISABELLE: Armand and I often said: if we could have stopped you, your life would have been different.

(MARY *nods ruefully.*)

MARY: Yes. But not necessarily better.

INT. MARY'S OFFICE. DAY

MARY *looks up as* AIKO *enters the office looking distraught. Dialogue in English.*

MARY: What is it?

AIKO: Katsugi has been arrested.

MARY: What for?

AIKO: They're rounding up anyone who's supposed to be subversive. Orders of the secret service.

(*She slumps into a chair opposite* MARY, *who's frowning in thought.*)

MARY: I'm sorry.

(*Silence. Then* AIKO *speaks, a touch tentatively.*)

AIKO: Is General Masuda's wife still one of your customers?

(MARY *looks at her, alarmed.*)

MARY: I can't ask her to approach him. He wouldn't take any notice if she did.

AIKO: What about Kurihama?

MARY: Kentaro? What could he do?

AIKO: He's a General, isn't he?

(MARY *continues to look at her, her expression dubious.*)

INT. STUDY IN MARY'S HOUSE. EVENING

KENTARO KURIHAMA, *now in his sixties, but still by all appearances youthful and vigorous, sits contemplating* MARY *for a moment in silence, before he speaks. Eventually he shakes his head.*

KENTARO: I'm sorry, you must tell Aiko I can do nothing for her husband this time.

MARY: Is there a reason?

(KENTARO *doesn't answer, but his brow furrows in irritation.*)

I know you don't like discussing these things, I know it's not the done thing to talk to women about politics, but I would like to know why everyone is so jumpy. Including you.

(KENTARO *sighs and says nothing for a while. Then he turns to her.*)

KENTARO: Everything is very complicated. So what I'm telling you is quite crudely simplified. Basically, there are two factions in the Army. One is in favour of war with Russia again. The other prefers the idea of a temporary alliance with Russia, so that we can continue our expansion in China.

MARY: And which faction do you belong to?

KENTARO: I do my duty.

MARY: That's not an answer to the question, is it?

(KENTARO *looks away for a moment. He's clearly reluctant to expand.*)

KENTARO: I do not belong to either side. I am not a believer in the benefits of war. My position is therefore . . . somewhat isolated.

MARY: That's why you can't do anything to help.

KENTARO: I am already vulnerable to criticism. The defence of a Socialist agitator . . .

MARY: He's not an agitator, he's a loudmouth.

KENTARO: All right, the defence of a Socialist loudmouth would be a useless gesture which might weaken my standing still further.

(*Silence.* MARY *is not especially pleased with this reasoning.*)

MARY: Why do you suppose this country is so anxious to fight with all its neighbours?

(KENTARO *considers for a moment before answering.*)

KENTARO: Perhaps we have been friends with you British long enough to think: why shouldn't we have an Empire?

EXT. IMPERIAL HOTEL. NIGHT. 1936
MARY *leaves the hotel in the early evening, wrapped up against the cold. She makes her way to the Dodge through flurries of snow.*

EXT. MARY'S HOUSE. NIGHT
The snow is still falling; it's quite deep in MARY'S *garden. Once the image is established, there's some unexpected peripheral movement, and the indistinct figure of a man in a greatcoat crosses a*

moonlit strip of the garden, moving from one shadow to a deeper
shadow.

INT. BEDROOM IN MARY'S HOUSE. NIGHT
KENTARO is already asleep between the quilts. MARY puts her book
aside, looks down at him for a moment, then reaches out to switch
off the lights. She settles down in the darkness, hearing the wind
howling outside.

EXT. MARY'S HOUSE. NIGHT
The house, shrouded in swirling snow. There's a blizzard in
progress.

INT. BEDROOM. NIGHT
MARY jerks awake as the bedroom door crashes back on its hinges.
There's a huge man in the doorway with a drawn sword. He's there
for a second, getting his bearings and then he lunges forward, the
sword flashing down and biting into the quilt where KENTARO's
head had been, a second before.
KENTARO dives for his clothes as the assassin recovers his balance,
retrieves the sword and moves towards him, raising it once again.
MARY catches at his foot and trips him, which gives KENTARO just
sufficient time to fetch his service revolver out of his jacket, cock it
and fire it point-blank at the assassin, who goes down like a tree
trunk.
KENTARO moves swiftly round the room to turn the light on. He
drops to one knee beside MARY, putting down the revolver and
taking her hands in his.
KENTARO, from MARY's point of view.
KENTARO: Are you all right?
    (Before she can answer, a second assassin with a sword appears
    in the doorway behind KENTARO. MARY cries out. The
    assassin raises his sword; another shot rings out from the
    corridor outside. The assassin falls to his knees and the man in
    the greatcoat appears in the doorway and deals the assassin a
    tremendous blow with the butt of his revolver. The assassin
    crashes forward on to his stomach.
    There's a pause and then KENTARO barks at the man,
    TAKASHI MARUYAMA, in Japanese.)
Any more?

111

MARUYAMA: No, this is all.
KENTARO: Better late than never.
    (KENTARO *turns back to* MARY, *reverting to English*.)
    I don't believe you've met Mr Maruyama, my bodyguard.
    (MARUYAMA *interrupts, in Japanese*.)
MARUYAMA: I think we'd better get out of here.
KENTARO: Yes.
MARUYAMA: You get dressed. I'll wait outside.
    (*He leaves the room abruptly.*
    MARY, *meanwhile, has been recovering her wits*.)
MARY: The shop's the best place to go.
KENTARO: No.
MARY: We'll go in my car.

INT. DODGE. NIGHT
MARY *moves closer to* KENTARO *on the back seat of the Dodge,
which* MARUYAMA *is driving. Uncharacteristically,* KENTARO
reaches out to put his arm round her.

EXT. IMPERIAL HOTEL. NIGHT
The Dodge pulls up outside the Imperial hotel.

INT. MARY'S OFFICE. DAWN
KENTARO *is on the telephone, speaking in Japanese.*
MARY *watches him from an armchair.*
KENTARO: No, I can't give you my number. I don't know
    where I'm going to be. I'll call you later today at the
    Ministry.
    (*He puts the telephone down and, after a moment's reflection,
    speaks to* MARY *in English*.)
    A lot of people have been killed. They've occupied the
    General Staff HQ. There are hundreds of them on the
    streets. Search parties.
MARY: Who are they?
KENTARO: Junior officers. The war party.
MARY: And who are they looking for?
KENTARO: Anyone in opposing cliques, anyone . . . moderate.
    Old men. They want to get rid of the old men.
MARY: What will happen?
    (KENTARO *shakes his head and shrugs his shoulders*.)

You must stay here.

KENTARO: Perhaps. I must think.

(*Silence. Then* KENTARO *looks up at her miserably.*)

They also broke into my house.

MARY: And what happened?

KENTARO: Some damage. But it seems my wife is safe.

(*He looks down again. Silence.*)

She's been very ill, you know.

MARY: No, I didn't know.

KENTARO: Well, she has.

(MARY's *about to speak, but she's cut off as* KENTARO *rises to his feet.*)

There's a back entrance, yes?

MARY: Yes.

KENTARO: Show me where it is. Then I must make some more telephone calls.

(*He looks up at her.*)

I'm afraid this is only the beginning.

INT. DINING-ROOM IN ALICIA BASSETT-HILL'S HOUSE. DAY. 1938

MARY *looks down somewhat queasily at the overdone roast beef and two vegetables on her plate.*

She is lunching with ALICIA, *now well over seventy, who chews away placidly for some time before being in a position to speak.*

ALICIA: I don't know how many times I've explained to her how to make Yorkshire pudding, she still hasn't the least idea.

MARY: I'm not sure I can remember what Yorkshire pudding's supposed to taste like.

ALICIA: Not like this, that's for certain.

MARY: Well, it's . . . very nice, anyway.

ALICIA: No, it isn't.

(*Silence. Then* ALICIA *looks up at* MARY, *eyes narrowed.*)

I don't believe I've ever asked you, Mary, do you believe in God?

MARY: Not particularly.

ALICIA: No, I'm not altogether sure I do any more.

(MARY *is extremely surprised.*)

113

I don't see it makes any more sense than what they believe,
do you?

MARY: Well, no.

ALICIA: In which case, it's probably just as well I made so few
converts.

MARY: Well, yes, if you look at it that way.

(ALICIA *goes on eating for a moment, in silence*.)

ALICIA: On the other hand, I haven't entirely lost hope that
God has some specific task in mind for me.

(*She smiles, reaching across to pour* MARY *some more wine*.)

INT. MARY'S SHOP. DAY

As MARY *emerges from her office, she is intercepted by* AIKO, *who
has been sitting waiting for her*.

AIKO: Have you got a moment?

MARY: Of course. Why didn't you let me know? Have you been
waiting long?

AIKO: I didn't know if you'd heard about Countess Kurihama.

MARY: Heard what?

AIKO: She died.

(MARY *stands there for a moment, too stunned to react,
remembering*.)

INT. CHANGING-ROOM AT TSUSHIMAYA. DAY

MARY *takes measurements, acutely aware that the* COUNTESS *is
watching her carefully in the mirror*.

INT. MARY'S SHOP. DAY

MARY *shakes her head, still in shock*.

EXT. MARY'S HOUSE. EVENING

It is towards sunset.

MARY *opens the door to* KENTARO *herself. After a moment of
surprise, he leans forward to kiss her on the cheek*.

MARY: Come in.

INT. STUDY IN MARY'S HOUSE. EVENING

MARY *is watching* KENTARO, *but he seems much as ever; perhaps a
little lighter than usual. He turns to her*.

KENTARO: Can it really be true, you have lived in Japan
    more than thirty years, and you have still never seen
    Nikko?
MARY: No, I haven't.
KENTARO: Wouldn't you like to? I have four days' leave. It's
    beautiful in the spring.
    (MARY *smiles, pleased.*)
MARY: Shall we take the car?
KENTARO: No. Let's go on our own.

EXT. HOTEL. DAWN
*A Japanese hotel at the foot of Mount Nantai on the shores of Lake
Chuzenji. Springtime.*

INT. NANTAI HOTEL ROOM. DAWN
MARY *wakes to see* KENTARO, *framed in the window, looking out
at Mount Nantai. He hears her stirring and turns back to her,
smiling.*

EXT. ROAD BELOW CHUZENJI. DAY
*An elderly bus negotiates the astonishing series of hairpin bends
leading down from Chuzenji towards Nikko.*

INT. BUS. DAY
MARY *is jerked towards* KENTARO *as the bus takes another bend.
She laughs, bracing herself against the next one.*

EXT. TOSHOGU SHRINE. DAY
MARY *and* KENTARO *stand in front of the astonishing riot of
baroque decoration, which is the Yomei-mon Gate.
Eventually, he turns to her.*
KENTARO: What do you think?
MARY: Well, it's more impressive than sympathetic.
    (KENTARO *nods, agreeing.*)

EXT. AVENUE OF CRYPTOMERIAS. DAY
MARY *and* KENTARO *walk arm in arm between giant cryptomeria
trees. The sun slants down between the austere trunks, dappling the
path ahead of them.*

115

INT. MAIN DINING-ROOM IN THE HOTEL. EVENING
The meal is over, everything cleared away except the tea and sake,
and MARY *and* KENTARO *have been left on their own.*

MARY: Are they going to send you back to China?

KENTARO: I don't know. Probably not. I think my campaigning days are over.

MARY: You have been there, though, haven't you?

KENTARO: Last year, yes.

MARY: Well, what's happening over there?
(KENTARO *hesitates, his expression troubled.*)
I know you hate to talk about these things.

KENTARO: Discretion is a habit.

MARY: But what did happen in Nanking?
(KENTARO *is profoundly uneasy. He pours some more sake,*
frowning ferociously. Eventually he speaks.)

KENTARO: When we fought with all those European Armies to put down the Boxer Rebellion, we were shocked by their conduct, the looting, the indiscipline, the casual brutality. We thought this was not a way for soldiers to behave. But in Nanking . . . I saw things . . . I could never have believed. Our army, even quite high-ranking officers, behaved like animals. Animals. It was as if we had learned . . . your barbarity, and were trying to make it perfect. It was not to be recognized as the army which I joined.
(*Silence.* MARY *is impressed by his seriousness. Her response is quiet.*)

MARY: Then perhaps you should resign.

KENTARO: We do not resign. There is no machinery for resignation.

MARY: But surely . . . at your age . . .

KENTARO: As long as I am required by my country, I must serve.

MARY: Even if your country begins to go insane?

KENTARO: I may think my thoughts: but my body belongs to the Emperor. I will give advice when it is sought: but if the advice is rejected, the adviser keeps silent and obeys.
(*Silence.*)

MARY: It's a very difficult country to understand.

KENTARO: Not if you are born here.
(MARY *looks away, biting her lip.*)

116

EXT. TOSHOGU SHRINE. DAY
MARY *and* KENTARO *are back at the shrine; he leads her through the Sakashita-mon Gate.*
KENTARO: I hope you may find this more to your taste.

EXT. STAIRWAY. DAY
MARY *pauses as* KENTARO *talks to a Shinto priest at the foot of an immense stairway. Eventually, he joins her.*
KENTARO: He's not supposed to let us go to the tomb
    unaccompanied . . .
MARY: Oh?
KENTARO: But he has made an exception.

EXT. STAIRWAY. DAY
The stairway winds up through giant cryptomerias. MARY *pauses to look back down at the roofs and courtyards of the shrine.*
KENTARO: Tired?
MARY: No, just looking.
    (*She looks up at him.*)
    Three years at Tsushimaya gave me very strong calves.

EXT. IEYASU'S TOMB. DAY
The quiet tomb behind the little shrine has an entirely different atmosphere from the principal buildings below. MARY *clearly responds to its weather-beaten simplicity. A long shot through the gates shows her inspecting the cylindrical tower in which Ieyasu is buried. Another angle shows* KENTARO, *his back to the sarcophagus, looking out through the trees.*
After a while, MARY *comes over to join him.*
MARY: It's beautiful.
KENTARO: Very calm, yes?
    (*She turns to look back at the sarcophagus.*)
MARY: Tell me about Ieyasu.
KENTARO: He was the first Tokugawa Shogun. He probably did
    more than anyone to make the Japanese what we are today.
    He died the same week as Shakespeare.
MARY: Really?
KENTARO: He was suspicious of foreigners. He closed the
    country to them. Except for one. The first Englishman who

ever visited Japan. Will Adams. He liked him so much, he
wouldn't allow him to go home.

MARY: And did Will Adams want to go home?

KENTARO: In the end he got used to living with us.
(*Silence. Then* KENTARO *takes* MARY's *hand.*)
Did you know that my wife had died?

MARY: Yes, I did. I'm sorry.

KENTARO: She was a very good wife.

MARY: I met her once, you know.

KENTARO: Yes. That was wrong of her. When I found out, I
made her cancel her order.

MARY: Oh, that was you.

KENTARO: Yes.

MARY: You needn't have. Once the clothes were made, she
might as well have had them.

KENTARO: I knew every time I looked at them, I would have
thought of you.
(*Silence.*)
Would you like to marry me?
(MARY *is taken completely by surprise. She closes her eyes for a
moment.*)

MARY: If I say yes, would you tell our son? Would we be able to
see him?
(KENTARO *is surprised in his turn; he considers very carefully.*)

KENTARO: No.
(*He lets go of her hand, she lowers her eyes.*)

MARY: In that case, I think we should just go on as we are.
(KENTARO *turns away and looks out through the trees for a
moment. He's evidently bitterly disappointed. Eventually, he
mumbles a reply.*)

KENTARO: As you like.
(*The two of them, not looking at each other, Ieyasu's tomb in
the background.*)

EXT. PRECINCTS OF THE ASAKUSA KANNON TEMPLE. NIGHT
*The stream of pilgrims with lanterns flows towards the temple. It's
the Festival of the Dead. Among them is* MARY, *alone this time,
dressed in black, her expression solemn.*
It's 1941, and the atmosphere is radically different from the time of
MARY's *first visit in 1905. For one thing the pilgrims are nearly all*

women; there are hardly any men and very few children. The mood
of the crowd is sombre and there is very little of the exuberant
commerce normally surrounding the participants in the festival.

EXT. KOTOTOI BRIDGE. NIGHT
MARY *watches, her expression melancholy, as the wood and paper
boats with their miniature lanterns are sent off down the river. She
looks up to see a woman staring at her coldly and, gradually but
unmistakably, becomes aware that the women on the bridge are
directing towards her a very real wave of hostility. She tries to smile
at the first woman, who does not react in any way.*
MARY *begins to feel nervous, alone in the crowd.*

EXT. BANKS OF THE SUMIDA RIVER. DAY
MARY'*s first day in Tsukiji: she walks along the bank, looking at
the river below.*
MISAO *follows, at a discreet distance. Passers-by stare curiously at*
MARY, *not acknowledging her. From time to time the word 'ijin' is
heard.*

EXT. KOTOTOI BRIDGE. NIGHT
Aware now of her vulnerable position, MARY *begins to try to leave
the bridge. The crowd seems unyielding.* MARY *is squeezed and
jostled by women whose expressions vary from coldly indifferent to
fiercely angry.*

EXT. APPROACHES TO KOTOTOI BRIDGE. NIGHT
MARY, *out of breath now, slightly panicked, manages to force her
way off the bridge.*

EXT. TEMPLE PRECINCTS. NIGHT
MARY *hurries against the stream of visitors to the festival, more than
ever aware of and frightened by the hostility of the crowd.*

INT. DODGE. NIGHT
MARY *scrambles into her car, slams the door behind her, puts her
hands across the wheel and rests her forehead on the back of her
hands.*

EXT. MARY'S HOUSE. EVENING
A winter's evening. Blustery rain.

INT. STUDY IN MARY'S HOUSE. EVENING
MARY *faces* KENTARO *across the coffee table.*
MARY: I don't want to leave. Where would I go?
KENTARO: America?
MARY: Why should I want to go to America?
KENTARO: Because I cannot guarantee your safety.
MARY: What's happening?
(*Silence.* KENTARO *looks round the room.*)
KENTARO: I don't know. I am no longer . . . at the centre of
        things. But I see enough to guess how critical they are.
MARY: If the worst happened, war, I suppose I'd be interned?
KENTARO: Maybe.
(*Silence.*)
MARY: I think I would rather take the risk.
KENTARO: Well, will you at least spend some time in
        Karuizawa? Most of the diplomats have been transferred up
        there.
MARY: Well, when should I go?
KENTARO: Tomorrow.
MARY: What will you do?
KENTARO: As always. Say what I think, and do as I'm told.

EXT. MARY'S CHALET IN KARUIZAWA. DAY
It's early morning on a cold, clear winter's day.

INT. CHALET. DAY
MARY, *in her warm European dressing gown and slippers, moves to
the front door and picks up her Japanese-language newspaper. She's
moving away from the door when something on the back page
catches her eye. It's a photograph of Pearl Harbor after the attack,
surrounded by huge banner headlines. She stands there, staring at it,
paralysed.*

INT. MAIN ROOM OF THE CHALET. DAY
MARY *sits by the fire, still in her dressing gown, nursing a cup of*

tea. The radio is on. Among the excited observations of the Japanese announcer, the words 'Pearl Harbor' stand out clearly. MARY *listens, appalled.*

INT. MARY'S OFFICE. DAY. 1942
MARY *sits, facing, across her desk,* MINAGAWA SAN, *now well into her fifties and an impeccably elegant figure, in spite of her surplus weight, and* TAKASHI OKAMATO, *her lawyer, a Westernized forty-year-old, who is handing her some papers. Dialogue in Japanese.*
TAKASHI: This is the deed of gift transferring ownership in your companies to Minagawa San, if you'd like to sign it.
   (MARY *takes the document.*)
   And we were going to speak about changing the name of your shops. I don't believe we can expect to do very much business under an English name.
MARY: It isn't an English name, but I take your point.
MINAGAWA: I know the Mackenzie trademark is very well known but . . .
MARY: But you think Minagawa would be a more prudent name to trade under.
MINAGAWA: I didn't say that.
   (*Silence, as* MARY *contemplates. Finally, she smiles ruefully.*)
MARY: Oh, why not?
   (*She signs the deed of gift.*)
MINAGAWA: This is only a formality, a purely temporary measure.
MARY: What's going to change it?
TAKASHI: Well, one can't exactly predict . . .
MARY: The outcome of the war?
   (*The telephone rings.* MARY *lifts the receiver.*)
   Hello.
   (*She listens for a while, her expression grave. Then she speaks in English.*)
   I'll be over there as quickly as I can.

INT. LIVING-ROOM IN ALICIA BASSETT-HILL'S HOUSE. DAY
Two impassive soldiers wait in the corners of the room. On the central table is a small open suitcase.
MARY *watches, concerned, as* ALICIA, *now about eighty, moves*

slowly back from her bookshelves holding a small, dog-eared black volume.

ALICIA: Better pack my hymn book, I'm sure to be needing that.

MARY: If you forget anything, I can get it over to you.

(ALICIA *smiles at her affectionately.*)

ALICIA: Won't they be coming for you soon?

MARY: I don't know. I suppose so. But I'll find out where you are and get in touch with you.

ALICIA: I have a feeling it's not going to be as easy as that.

(ALICIA *has a last look at her suitcase's contents, then closes it up.*)

But I do hope at last I can be of some use.

MARY: What do you mean?

ALICIA: I'm so close to the end of my life, I don't really mind what happens. So perhaps I can be of some help to those who do mind.

(*One of the soldiers has stepped forward, and now takes her case.*)

EXT. ALICIA BASSETT-HILL'S HOUSE. DAY
A covered lorry waits outside the house, the tail-gate opened, a number of soldiers lounging about in the vicinity.
ALICIA *is conducted towards the lorry, walking arm-in-arm with*
MARY.

ALICIA: Do you know, it's a stange thing, I still love this country.

MARY: Take care.

ALICIA: I've always admired your spirit, my dear.

MARY: You've been very kind to me.

ALICIA: Goodbye.

(*She says this so suddenly, it takes* MARY *by surprise.
Two of the soldiers manhandle her into the truck, and a soldier throws her suitcase in after her. The tail-gate is banged shut and the darkness swallows* ALICIA *up.*
MARY *stands on the pavement, chewing at her lip.*)

INT. STUDY IN MARY'S HOUSE. DAY
AIKO *sits, waiting, as* MARY *stands, looking out of the window.*
MARY: Well, Aiko, it's this.

(*She turns back to look at* AIKO, *whose expression is slightly apprehensive.*)
I've no means of knowing how long I've got: so I think you'd better have the house.

AIKO: What?

MARY: Otherwise they'll probably simply confiscate it. I'd much rather you had it.

AIKO: I don't know if I . . .

MARY: You like it, don't you?

AIKO: It's a beautiful house.

MARY: I know anything that could be construed as political activity is impossible at the moment, but you could use the house as a base: to prepare for what might be done to help women after the war. Or just live here if you want to.

AIKO: I don't know what to say.

MARY: Let me stay for as long as I'm allowed to stay; and I'd want you to promise to keep on Toba San, I don't think she has anywhere else to go.

AIKO: Of course.
(*Silence.* AIKO *frowns in thought.*)
What about rent?

MARY: I don't want rent: if I did, I know you very likely couldn't pay it. I just want the house looked after and lived in.

AIKO: And used to some purpose.

MARY: If you can. But carefully, for God's sake.
(*She approaches* AIKO *and sits down next to her.*)
You'll do it, won't you?

AIKO: You'll have to let me think about it.

MARY: I'll get Takashi to draw up the papers.
(*She takes* AIKO'*s hand and kisses it.*)

EXT. GARDEN OF KURIHAMA'S HOUSE. DAY
MARY *opens the gate and stands for a moment, remembering.*

EXT. GARDEN. NIGHT
The moonlit garden, as it was when she first saw it. KENTARO *turns away from her and she watches him disappearing back into the house.*

123

EXT. KURIHAMA'S HOUSE. DAY
A panel slides back, and KENTARO, *backlit from within the house, stands in the entrance.* MARY *hurries over to him and he embraces her. Then he closes the panel behind them.*

INT. DRAWING-ROOM IN KURIHAMA'S HOUSE. DAY
A magnificently elegant room, in which KENTARO, *in his* yukata, *fits the setting far better than* MARY, *who seems agitated and ill at ease.* KENTARO *indicates the room with a sweeping gesture.*
KENTARO: What do you think?
> (*She doesn't answer. She's too anxious to know what's going on.*)
MARY: Is there any news?
> (KENTARO *sighs, regretful at being brought so abruptly to earth.*)
KENTARO: If I'm not very much mistaken, I believe my days at the Ministry are numbered.
MARY: And what will happen?
KENTARO: I'll be moved to somewhere . . . out at the edge, where my opinions won't cause any embarrassment.
MARY: Which means you won't be able to do any more for me.
> (*Silence.*)
KENTARO: While I'm still at the Ministry, I might be able to arrange passage for you out of the country: once they get rid of me . . .
MARY: But I don't want to leave the country.
KENTARO: You might have to spend years in some internment camp.
MARY: I'll take my chances.
KENTARO: At least let me . . .
MARY: No.
> (KENTARO *gives up: He smiles at* MARY.)
KENTARO: I wanted you to see inside my house before . . .
MARY: Before what?
KENTARO: I just wanted you to see my house.

INT. BEDROOM IN KENTARO'S HOUSE. NIGHT
MARY *is asleep in* KENTARO's *arms. He lies, his eyes wide open, staring into space, pensive.*

124

INT. BREAKFAST-ROOM IN MARY'S HOUSE. DAY
MARY and AIKO are eating breakfast when TOBA hurries into the room, ashen, speaking in Japanese.
TOBA: There are soldiers here.
MARY: Then show them in.
(*TOBA leaves the room, flustered, and MARY turns to AIKO and speaks in English.*)
This must be for me.
(*TOBA shows four soldiers in uniform into the room before AIKO can answer. The spokesman bows politely to MARY. Dialogue in Japanese.*)
1ST DEPORTATION OFFICER: Mackenzie San?
MARY: Yes.
1ST DEPORTATION OFFICER: Would you please pack two suitcases, not too large, and be ready to leave the house in an hour?
MARY: Why?
1ST DEPORTATION OFFICER: We have to put you on board a neutral ship at pier number one. It sails at noon.
(*MARY frowns incredulously, trying to take this in.*)
MARY: Sails for where?
1ST DEPORTATION OFFICER: London.
MARY: There must be some mistake.
1ST DEPORTATION OFFICER: No mistake. We have orders.
MARY: I'd like to make a phone call.
1ST DEPORTATION OFFICER: I'm very sorry, this is not permitted.
MARY: Wait a minute, are you sure you . . . ?
1ST DEPORTATION OFFICER: You'd better do your packing. We can't leave any later than nine o'clock.
(*MARY looks at him, at a loss for words.*)

INT. DRAWING-ROOM. DAY
Impulsively, MARY is packing the shogi board and its pieces; half-way through the process she stops.
Dialogue in English.
MARY: This is absurd.
AIKO: No, take it, you must take it.
(*MARY tips the rest of the pieces into the suitcase and closes it.*

125

TOBA *and the policemen, discreet presences in the corners of the room, watch her.*)
MARY: I don't want you to come to the dock, Aiko, I'd rather say goodbye here.
AIKO: Are you sure?
MARY: Yes.
(MARY *searches in her handbag.*)
I've written a cheque for Toba. See she cashes it today.
AIKO: I can look after her.
MARY: No, I want to do this.
(*She finds the cheque, tears it off and crosses to hand it to* TOBA. TOBA *looks at it, bewildered, as* MARY *speaks to her in Japanese.*)
The Baroness will stay here with you. I'll be back as soon as I can.
(TOBA *nods miserably as* MARY *turns to the policemen's spokesman.*)
We may as well go.
(*As two of the policemen step forward to take* MARY's *suitcases,* TOBA *pulls her apron up to cover her face and bursts into noisy tears.* MARY *is trying very hard to control herself.*)

EXT. MARY'S HOUSE. DAY
A beautiful summer's day. MARY *turns to* AIKO.
Dialogue in English.
MARY: I will come back.
AIKO: Of course.
MARY: And you'll be careful, won't you?
AIKO: Don't worry.
MARY: Because I'm sure, when this is all over, things are going to change. And you must be there.
(*She embraces* AIKO, *kissing her on both cheeks.*)
Thank you for everything.
AIKO: Safe journey.
(*She wants to say more, but can't.*
MARY *is led away by the soldiers. Halfway down the path, she breaks away from them, snaps a leaf from the ginger tree, crushes it and inhales the scent. Then she follows the soldiers to their car: one of them holds open the back door.* MARY *glances back once at* AIKO *and* TOBA *standing in the doorway.*)

126

INT. MILITARY CAR. DAY
MARY *is sandwiched between two policemen in the back seat. She
leans forward to be able to look out of the window.*

EXT. YOKOHAMA STREET. DAY
*Away in the distance, hanging over the city, visible in the sharp-
edged clarity of the morning is the snow-covered summit of Mount
Fuji.*

INT. MILITARY CAR. DAY
MARY *sits back in her seat and sniffs at the leaf she's still holding.
Her expression is composed, but tears begin to spill from her eyes.*

INT. CUSTOMS SHED. DAY
MARY's *luggage has been checked through and she's moving towards
the exit leading on to the pier, when* KENTARO *arrives, breathless
with haste. She sees him at the entrance to the customs shed, and
runs over towards him.*
The soldier at her elbow hurries after her, but a sharp word from
KENTARO *when* MARY *reaches him is enough to make the soldiers
retire to a respectful distance.*
KENTARO *and* MARY *stand looking at one another, isolated amidst
the bustle of departure.*
KENTARO: I'm glad I caught you, I couldn't have come on the
    boat. Apparently, it's full of reporters.
MARY: I told you I didn't want to leave.
KENTARO: You don't know what the internment camps are like.
    I thought I had better make the decision for you.
MARY: Again.
    (*Silence. Then* KENTARO *nods ruefully.*)
KENTARO: I hope finally you will find it a correct decision.
    (MARY *continues to look sceptical.*)
    I also will be going on a journey soon.
MARY: Where to?
KENTARO: I don't know.
    (MARY *looks at him, puzzled by his tone.*)
    There is nothing to say, is there, after all this time?
MARY: No.
KENTARO: But I didn't want you to leave without a goodbye.

(KENTARO *looks around at the slowly emptying shed.*)
It is best to leave, you know.
MARY: I don't understand why any of this is happening.
KENTARO: A year ago it didn't seem possible that Germany
would not win; so we wanted our share. And when a
country wants badly enough to go on the attack, it hardly
matters to them who they choose: anyone will do. I'm just
sorry it turns out to be your country.
MARY: My former country.
KENTARO: Your country.
(MARY *looks at him for a moment.*)
MARY: There isn't anything you want to tell me, is there?
(KENTARO *doesn't answer for a while. Then he shakes his
head.*)
KENTARO: No.
MARY: I just wondered.
(*At this point a soldier steps forward, speaking in Japanese.*)
2ND DEPORTATION OFFICER: I think it's time to embark, if
you'll forgive me, General.
KENTARO: One moment.
(*The soldier withdraws again, bowing.*)
MARY: I'm going to come back as soon as it's possible.
KENTARO: Ah, yes?
MARY: So I will see you again.
KENTARO: Perhaps. I don't think we should count on it.
MARY: No?
KENTARO: I think we should imagine this will be our last
meeting.
(*He takes her in his arms.*)
And say goodbye.
(*He kisses her. She clings to him for a moment and then breaks
away abruptly and hurries towards the exit.
In the doorway* MARY *glances back at him briefly, and then
disappears.*
KENTARO *doesn't move for quite some time.*)

EXT. SINGAPORE HARBOUR. DAY
The MS Gripsholm, *a Swedish freighter, is riding at anchor in the
harbour. It's August 1942. The sun blazes down.*

INT. MARY'S CABIN. DAY
MARY *lies on her bunk in her underwear, fanning herself with a
magazine. A knock at the door.* MARY *scrambles into her* yukata
and opens the door. The Swedish purser waits respectfully outside.
MARY: Come in. What is it?
> (*The purser steps into the cabin.*)
PURSER: The Japanese Occupation Authorities wish to send a
> man aboard to interview you.
MARY: What about?
PURSER: I'm afraid I have no idea, but they insist.
MARY: Can't I refuse?
PURSER: They could overrun this ship in five minutes, if they
> were so inclined. Why don't you see their officer in the
> main lounge?
> (MARY *sighs, frowning worriedly.*)
> We need to leave Singapore in a few hours. Please don't
> make difficulties.

INT. PASSENGERS' LOUNGE. DAY
MARY *sits on her own, waiting apprehensively. There are a number
of other passengers in the lounge.* MARY *watches the door.*

INT. KURIHAMA'S OFFICE IN THE WAR MINISTRY. DAY
KENTARO *is clearing his desk. A number of cardboard boxes stand
by the door. He is evidently in the process of vacating his office.*

INT. PASSENGERS' LOUNGE. DAY
MARY *looks up sharply. Standing in the doorway is a Japanese
officer in his thirties,* CAPTAIN NOBUSHIGE OZAKI. *His highly
polished boots, his sword, on which his hand lightly rests, his
brutally cropped hair, make of him an alarming figure.*
MARY *watches as the Swedish steward hurries over to him and then
points out* MARY. *The passengers have all fallen silent. They watch
as the captain crosses to speak to* MARY.
OZAKI: Mackenzie San?
MARY: Yes.
OZAKI: I am Captain Nobushige Ozaki.
MARY: What can I do for you?
OZAKI: May I sit?
MARY: Please do.

(OZAKI *moves a chair – chained to the floor like all the others – and settles himself in it.*)

OZAKI: Not as hot in here, I'm pleased to say.

MARY: Hot enough.

OZAKI: Many of us are finding the climate in Malaya difficult to get used to.

MARY: I imagine.

OZAKI: Tea?

MARY: No, thank you.

(*Silence.* MARY's *politeness is formal to the point of frostiness.* MARY *is aware of the other passengers' eyes upon her.* OZAKI *seems slightly at a loss. Eventually he speaks again.*)

OZAKI: I am here on behalf of Lieutenant-General Count Kurihama.

(MARY *looks up at him, startled.*)

EXT. KURIHAMA'S HOUSE. DAY

KENTARO *lingers in the garden, moving slowly through it on his way towards the house.*

INT. PASSENGERS' LOUNGE. DAY

MARY *is puzzled, but relieved that this appears to be a social call.*

MARY: I saw the Count about three weeks ago.

OZAKI: Yes. But my message came from him yesterday.

MARY: I see.

OZAKI: He wanted me to find out if everything was satisfactory.

MARY: Perfectly, thank you.

OZAKI: And he hopes that you have forgiven him.

MARY: Let us say that, as always, I understand his position.

(*Silence. After a time,* OZAKI *produces a wallet from his inside pocket. He takes a photograph out of it and passes it across to* MARY. *Inset: a smiling woman and three children, a boy and two girls, standing in a garden, grouped around a stone lantern.* MARY *looks at the photograph, then up at* OZAKI *with wild surmise, then back at the photograph.*)

Your wife and children?

OZAKI: Yes.

(*She looks up at him for a moment.*)

MARY: Would you like to continue this conversation in my
    cabin?

INT. BEDROOM IN KURIHAMA'S HOUSE. EVENING
KENTARO *emerges from his bathroom, towelling himself vigorously,
his expression serene. Laid out meticulously on the bed is his dress
uniform.*

INT. MARY'S CABIN. DAY
OZAKI *hesitates in the doorway to the cabin.*
MARY: Don't worry. I'm not going to make a scene.
    (*He steps into the cabin and sits where indicated, in the cabin's
    one armchair.*
    MARY *perches on the stool in front of the dressing table.*)
    You must tell the Count I'm very grateful for this.
OZAKI: I will write. I never see him, you understand.
MARY: I didn't know.
    (*She looks at him for a moment, struggling to control herself.*)
    Where do you live?
OZAKI: Nagoya.
MARY: Have you always . . .?
OZAKI: Oh, yes, this is where my . . . parents come from. After
    the war you must visit.
    (MARY *shakes her head, smiling.*)
MARY: I was once offered a job in Nagoya.
OZAKI: Oh, yes?
MARY: I refused, I wanted to stay in Tokyo; I had some idea
    that what I was looking for might be there.
OZAKI: And was it?
MARY: It seems it was in Nagoya all along.
    (*Silence. She looks at him.*)

EXT. PRECINCTS OF THE ASAKUSA KANNON TEMPLE. NIGHT
The Festival of the Dead. The baby TARO *tugs at* MARY's *hair.*
MARY: (*Voice over*) I took you once, when you were a baby, to
    the Festival of the Dead. For some reason . . .

INT. MARY'S CABIN. DAY
OZAKI *listens intently, his expression impenetrable.*
MARY: . . . that evening is my most vivid memory of you.

OZAKI: I see.

MARY: What did you say your name was?

OZAKI: Ozaki Nobushige.

(*Silence. Then* OZAKI *smiles.*)

When you go back to Japan . . .

MARY: Yes.

OZAKI: You must visit again the Festival of the Dead. That's where you will find me.

MARY: What do you mean?

OZAKI: I am a pilot.

(*Silence.* MARY *grapples with the implications of this.*)

MARY: But . . .

OZAKI: I will be there.

(MARY *looks at him.*)

INT. DRAWING-ROOM IN KURIHAMA'S HOUSE. EVENING
KENTARO *sits cross-legged on the floor, his eyes closed. Then he seems suddenly to come to himself and reaches for some object loosely bound in silk, which is lying on the floor beside him. He unwraps it unhurriedly. It's a short, bright sword.*

EXT. DECK OF THE MS GRIPSHOLM. DAY
OZAKI *turns to* MARY *at the top of the gangplank and bows deeply.* MARY *is still exerting iron control, but her voice is a little ragged.*

MARY: I'm sorry you have to go so soon.

OZAKI: I regret I am on duty at four.

MARY: Have you been happy?

(*He looks at her for a moment before answering.*)

OZAKI: Thank you: I have had a very happy life.

(*He takes her hand, bows again and kisses it.*)

My respects. Please take the greatest care of your health.

(*He turns abruptly and sets off down the gangplank towards a launch which bobs at its foot.*

MARY'*s face: her eyes are full of tears.*

OZAKI'*s descending figure from* MARY'*s point of view, blurred and indistinct.*

MARY *wipes her eyes and stands looking down. The launch pulls away from the freighter.* OZAKI *settles himself in the back, putting on his forage cap to protect the back of his neck*

132

against the fierce sun. He turns and stiffly raises a hand. MARY
waves back.)

EXT. KOTOTOI BRIDGE. NIGHT
Hundreds of wood and paper lanterns bob away down the river.

EXT. DECK OF THE MS GRIPSHOLM. DAY
MARY *watches as the launch putters back towards the harbour.
She's poised to wave again: but* CAPTAIN OZAKI *does not look
back.*